The A

by Grace Franklin

Lang**Syne**

PUBLISHING

WRITING *to* REMEMBER

Lang**Syne**

PUBLISHING

WRITING *to* REMEMBER

Strathclyde Business Centre
120 Carstairs Street, Glasgow G40 4JD
Tel: 0141 554 9944 Fax: 0141 554 9955
E-mail: info@scottish-memories.co.uk
www.langsyneshop.co.uk

Printed by Thomson Litho, East Kilbride
© Lang Syne Publishers Ltd 2006
ISBN 1-85217-063-8
ISBN 978-1-85217-063-9

The Andersons

ARMS:
Argent, a saltire engrailed sable
between four mullets Gules.

TERRITORY:
Aberdeenshire, Fife and Badenoch.

Chapter one:

The origins of the clan system

by Rennie McOwan

The original Scottish clans of the Highlands and the great families of the Lowlands and Borders were gatherings of families, relatives, allies and neighbours for mutual protection against rivals or invaders.

Scotland experienced invasion from the Vikings, the Romans and English armies from the south.

The Norman invasion of what is now England also had an influence on land-holding in Scotland. Some of these invaders stayed on and in time became 'Scottish'.

The word clan derives from the Gaelic language term 'clann', meaning children, and it was first used many centuries ago as communities were formed around tribal lands in glens and mountain fastnesses.

The format of clans changed over the centuries, but at its best the chief and his family held the land on behalf of all, like trustees, and the ordinary clansmen and women believed they had a blood relationship with the founder of their clan.

There were two way duties and obligations.

An inadequate chief could be deposed and replaced by someone of greater ability.

Clan people had an immense pride in race. Their relationship with the chief was like adult children to a father and they had a real dignity.

The concept of clanship is very old and a more feudal notion of authority gradually crept in.

Pictland, for instance, was divided into seven principalities ruled by feudal leaders who were the strongest and most charismatic leaders of their particular groups.

By the sixth century the 'British' kingdoms of Strathclyde, Lothian and Celtic Dalriada (Argyll) had emerged and Scotland, as one nation, began to take shape in the time of King Kenneth MacAlpin.

Some chiefs claimed descent from ancient kings which may not have been accurate in every case.

By the twelfth and thirteenth centuries the clans and families were more strongly brought under the central control of Scottish monarchs.

Lands were awarded and administered more and more under royal favour, yet the power of the area clan chiefs was still very great.

The long wars to ensure Scotland's independence against the expansionist ideas of English monarchs extended the influence of some clans and reduced the lands of others.

Those who supported Scotland's greatest king, Robert the Bruce, were awarded the territories of the families who had opposed his claim to the Scottish throne.

In the Scottish Borders country - the notorious Debatable Lands - the great families built up a ferocious reputation for providing warlike men accustomed to raiding into England and occasionally fighting one another.

Chiefs had the power to dispense justice and to confiscate lands and clan warfare produced a society where martial virtues - courage, hardiness, tenacity - were greatly admired.

Gradually the relationship between the clans and the Crown became strained as Scottish monarchs became more orientated to life in the Lowlands and, on occasion, towards England.

The Highland clans spoke a different language, Gaelic, whereas the language of Lowland Scotland and the court was Scots and in more modern times, English.

Highlanders dressed differently, had different customs, and their wild mountain land sometimes seemed almost foreign to people living in the Lowlands.

It must be emphasised that Gaelic culture was very rich and story-telling, poetry, piping, the clarsach (harp) and other music all flourished and were greatly respected.

Highland culture was different from other parts of Scotland but it was not inferior or less sophisticated.

Central Government, whether in London or Edinburgh, sometimes saw the Gaelic clans as a challenge to their authority and some sent expeditions into the Highlands and west to crush the power of the Lords of the Isles.

Nevertheless, when the eighteenth century Jacobite Risings came along the cause of the Stuarts was mainly supported by Highland clans.

The word Jacobite comes from the Latin for James - Jacobus. The Jacobites want--ed to restore the exiled Stuarts to the throne of Britain.

The monarchies of Scotland and England became one in 1603 when King James VI of Scotland (1st of England) gained the English throne after Queen Elizabeth died.

The Union of Parliaments of Scotland and England, the Treaty of Union, took place in 1707.

Some Highland clans, of course, and

Lowland families opposed the Jacobites and supported the incoming Hanoverians.

After the Jacobite cause finally went down at Culloden in 1746 a kind of ethnic cleansing took place. The power of the chiefs was curtailed. Tartan and the pipes were banned in law.

Many emigrated, some because they wanted to, some because they were evicted by force. In addition, many Highlanders left for the cities of the south to seek work.

Many of the clan lands became home to sheep and deer shooting estates.

But the warlike traditions of the clans and the great Lowland and Border families lived on, with their descendants fighting bravely for freedom in two world wars.

Remember the men from whence you came, says the Gaelic proverb, and to that could be added the role of many heroic women.

The spirit of the clan, of having roots, whether Highland or Lowland, means much to thousands of people.

Chapter two:

Sons of Andrew

The clan Anderson are something of a mystery. They have an ancient, bonny, blue tartan, no chief and no place to call home.

For a family with a name so commonplace that it can be found in phone books from Stockholm to Auckland and Wisconsin to Warsaw, they have an elusive past and appear to have kept a low profile during times of war and struggle. Anderson is ninth in frequency of Scottish family surnames.

Most Andersons south of Aberdeen simply began to name themselves after Saint Andrew the patron saint of their country. In the north, they followed the tradition of taking the clan Chief's name and became "son of Andrew". In common with Scandinavian ways, the family tended to be footloose and to rely on first names. An Icelandic phone book today, for example, lists people not by their last name, but by their first name.

While arms were awarded to "Anderson of that Ilk" by the Lord Lyon in the 16th century, that family has never been identified. Sadly, as a result, there is no known clan Chief and the chieftanship has remained dormant. Yet from that point in time, when formal and legal recognition was given to the Andersons as an "honourable community", a clan chief could have been there to represent that family in civic duties and on public occasions. Without the vital leadership, the Andersons have done what they have always been good at, keeping quiet in the background minding their own business – usually very successfully.

As one Anderson put it "we prospered while the bannock burned". Thinkers rather than fighters, they have had the tendency to keep to themselves and not look for trouble. Their intellectual qualities have moved them towards words rather than wars.

The name Anderson means many things. One natural origin is from St Andrew, the patron saint of Scotland. Indeed it is his cross which features on the clan shield. In the Gaelic the clan name is Mac Ghillie Aindrais or Gilleandrais which translates as son of the servant of Andrew. A Ghillie is a servant. Or even simpler, MacAindrea which is straight forwardly translated as son of Andrew. Mac means son of, in Gaelic.

But a complicating factor is that the Ross Clan are known in Gaelic as Clann Andrais or Andrews Clan. It is easy to see how these various nomenclatures could be confused in any language. So whether followers of the saint or simply sons of Andrew or his servant, Anderson has many antecedents all of which could be correct.

Andersons or MacAndrews do appear to have a "cadet" sept of the Ross family. A sept is the Irish word for a division of a tribe. Cadet refers to important clansmen related by blood to the chief line but forming their own branch.

So while well connected within the Ross hierarchy, the Andersons had their own lineage, a vague allegiance to people of the same, or similar name, and a great facility for survival.

Following their Ross connections, the Andersons can claim ties to the Irish royal house of Tara.

The first recorded chief of the Rosses was one Fearchar Mac-an –t- Saigairt. He was the son of a priest. In the early days of the Celtic and the Roman church there were no celibacy laws. Fearchars's father was the priest of Applecross Abbey on the north west coast of Scotland where they were hereditary abbots. They, in turn, were related to the O'Beolins of the Irish House of Tara who were the hereditary abbots of Duncliff and descended from Cairbre, son of King Naill of the Nine Hostages.

Applecross Abbey was founded by St Malrubha in 673. This Abbot of Bangor was also a descendant of the Irish King Naill. Interestingly, the Applecross lands were inherited by a woman at one point. This was common Pictish practice.

Leaping forward in time to 1215, Ferchar the first chief of the clan Ross backed Alexander II as King over those tribes in Scotland which were being moulded together into a nation. In the chronicles of Melrose it is recorded that "he cut off the heads of the king's enemies". He was created Earl of Ross in 1234 for his brave deeds and loyalty to the King. The successive Earl of Ross is noted for his bravery too – at the battle of Bannockburn in 1314 and at Halidon Hill 1333.

There is no mention of Andersons fighting alongside these Rosses. But without doubt there would be sons of Andrew and followers of the Saint Andrew in the Ross camp.

Large numbers of the Anderson clan can be found in the north-east of Scotland from around 1540. The most prominent family branches being the Andersons of Dowhill in Aberdeenshire, the Andersons of Western Ardbeck in Banffshire and the Andersons who were lairds of Candacraig in Strathdon, Aberdeenshire.

Dominated by the much more powerful families Farquharson, Forbes and Gordon, these fertile lands provided a living from farming for many people. Smallholdings abounded which enabled the Andersons to live independently but still enjoy the benefits of protection, patronage and trade by being an accepted part of the larger clan. When it suited, they could blend into the scenery.

In the words of a 20th century Anderson "My grandfather told my father, and he told me that our family had changed their name from Macgregor to Campbell and then to Anderson, when it was felt that a change was called for."

Clan membership, as interpreted by families of the Highlands of Scotland, was a matter of convenience or expediency. It was something which was used and changed as politics or pragmatism dictated.

However, in the Borders where there are also strongholds of Andersons, a blood connection was the main requirement to claim clanship. Pockets thrive to this day in and around Denholm and at Tushielaw, a notable crossroads in the upper Ettrick which is complete with pub. In that hostelry, or any other in the Borders or the Highland homelands of the Clan there is a 50-50 chance that the man sitting alone in a corner, immersed in a book, is an Anderson.

But they didn't always manage to stay out of trouble.

With their association with the Clan Chattan from around 1400, the Andersons or MacAndrew clan did draw blood. Prior to the 14th century, Clan Chattan were largely unheard of. It evolved into a confederation or alliance of various clans, the Andersons being one. As power waxed and waned among the different families so the relationships altered and protection was given or sought. The Clan Chattan were dominant over the Andersons. And through this allegiance the Andersons were to be found in the bloody brawl at the North Inch in Perth with the Clan Kay.

During King Robert III's reign –1337 till 1406 – the Chattans and the Kays had many scores to settle. So a mighty battle was arranged to take place at the North Inch on the banks of the River Tay. Each clan selected 60 of their best warriors as their champions. Armed with bows, axes and swords they prepared to fight, watched by the King himself. Such an exceptional fight naturally brought huge crowds of common folk who took up vantage viewing positions from the safety of nearby high grounds.

Just before battle commenced, a man was found to be absent from the Chattan side. His place was taken by a smith from Perth called Henry Bow Anderson or Hal O' the Wynd. The battle was bloody and furious. By the end of the hours of fighting all the warriors were dead or wounded. The only man unscathed was the late substitute, Hal.

Andersons again got into bad company in the Badenoch area of the Grampian Highlands. In the Kinara manuscript of 1676 it is written that 'sick-like Donald MacGillandrish of the clan Andrish came out of Muidart.' This describes a move from Moidart to Badenoch of the MacGillandrish clan centuries before. They held lands at Badenoch for generations and their descendants settled in Connage of Petty. Through Anglicisation, the Gaelic name was eventually changed to MacAndrew.

While they settled in Badenoch in Inverness-shire, they had to contend with an unsavoury neighbour, the 'Wolf of Badenoch'. This unpleasant character collected a band of renegades, stole lands from the Bishop of Moray and in 1390 burned Elgin Cathedral. Following this he was ex-communicated. But the Wolf turned out to be Alexander, Earl of Buchan and a brother of King Robert III.

There is no way of identifying any Andersons who might have been directly involved in these forays, but a little gentle involvement in cattle rustling along the centuries would be in keeping with the times.

Cattle raids were commonplace in the Highlands for more than 300 years from the 14th century onwards. The authorities found it difficult to police the region because of the inaccessible nature of the land with the physical obstacles of mountains, lochs and rivers.

Chapter three:

Thieves and killers

Life for people in those regions was hard. There was little fertile ground available for crops. The economy was based mainly on rearing black cattle. Hunting and fishing were vital for survival. But with the harsh climate during long winter months, food was often scarce. So people were driven to stealing cattle from their neighbours. Such raids would even extend as far as the lowlands.

Such cattle rustling expeditions went on as late as 1670. In that year a member of the Anderson Clan –'Little' John MacAndrew was involved in what was to be one of the last such raids recorded.

An expert bowman, Ian Beag, as Little John's name is in Gaelic, was living in Dalnahtnich. He was a valued and dependable servant of William Mackintosh of Kellachie. One dark night a cattle thief called McDonnell of Achluach descended on the lands of Kilravock with his band of men. They drove away the cattle of the baron. When the alarm was raised they were quickly pursed by the tenants headed by Mackintosh accompanied by 'Little' John MacAndrew.

The story goes that the cattle thieves had settled for the night in a bothy on the heights of Strathdean. McAndrew shot an arrow into the hut and the McDonnel swiftly came out. He slipped and fell on a cow hide which had been placed at the door, hairy side down by the clever McAndrew. McAndrew's next arrow found its mark on the prone frame of McDonnell, killing him instantly.

Alarmed by the commotion, the next man came running out of the hut, and also slipped on the smooth cow hide. He was killed by Mackintosh's arrow. Then a shower of arrows cascaded into the bothy through the door, windows and thatch until every man of the Lochaber band of thieves was dead.

With the exception of a sleeping sentry, not a single man survived to carry the tale to Lochaber. The men of Lochaber swore to kill 'Little' John. But luckily for him, this oath was never realised.

Chapter four:

Great and gifted

The Anderson genes are more concerned with words than weapons. From the number of distinguished academics who can claim clanship through their name, it is clear the family has a facility for language and learning.

The family name crops up in a wide range of disciplines, especially during the Scottish Enlightenment of the 18th century, a period of great intellectual activity and vision.

Following the Reformation when the country changed from a Roman Catholic persuasion to Protestantism, a minister called Patrick Anderson was noted because of his non-conformity to Knox's sweeping Protestant reforms. For those sins, he was imprisoned on the bass rock off the East coast at the mouth of the Firth of Forth. His son, however, got on well with the establishment due to his more liberal views and less severe religious attitudes which were tolerated a generation later. The younger Anderson published pamphlets which were considered acceptable. But he seems to have suffered from a hot-tempered attitude similar to his father because it is recorded the son died of apoplexy around 1728.

One of the most famous Anderson Clan members was John who was born in 1726 and lived to the ripe old age of 70. He was a Professor of Natural Philosophy at Glasgow University and was known affectionately by his students as 'Jolly Jack Phosphorous' due to his habit of setting off phosphorus explosions during his own lectures. This remarkable thinker, teacher and inventor was responsible for starting what has become Strathclyde University in Glasgow

His legacy was a bequest – with precious little money – for a new university of a more liberal type to be set up in Glasgow and named after him. Radically, for those times, it was to give instruction to women as well as men. Anderson wanted these versed in science and fit to enter the up-and –coming world of trade, industry and commerce.

He considered an innovative, alternative, teaching curriculum was needed to offer to students. The older Scottish universities were badly in need of reform. He had graduated from Glasgow University himself at the age of 19 and was appointed Professor of Oriental Languages there when he was 28 but transferred to the Chair of Natural Philosophy a couple of years later.

His concern was to provide 'useful learning.' Within ten months of his death , more than 1000 students had been enrolled in the Anderson Institute. Half of them were women and they were being prepared for jobs as mechanics and artisans following Anderson's fundamental philosophy that 'knowledge should be used in the service of society.'

Two hundred years later his phrase 'useful learning' was the motto Strathclyde University used to celebrate its bicentenary. He would be proud of the fact that today

Strathclyde is the third largest University in Scotland, has around 14,000 students and 3500 staff, is renowned world-wide for its teaching and research and is in the world's top ten league among universities for the income it generates from inventions.

In other walks of life, the Anderson clan members have earned more than a passing mention. For instance, in 1748 the mentally unstable widow of a soldier returned to her home town of Elgin and promptly gave birth to a son in the lavatories of the great Elgin Cathedral – the Lantern of the North. This child grew to become none other than General Andrew Anderson who went to work for the East India Company and made his fortune.

He never forgot his humble beginnings because when he died he bequeathed a considerable portion of his fortune to the town to care for people like is mother in poor and distressing circumstances. His Anderson's Institute was opened in 1833 and was designed by the architect who created St Giles Cathedral in Edinburgh.

Sited in Elgin town centre, the Institute provided a home for destitute children and old folk aged over 55 and a free school as well.

Another who left something worthwhile to Scots – particularly those in Edinburgh – was Patrick a physician who returned from studying in Venice with a cure-for-all remedy. These famous Anderson's Pills were manufactured in the Capital's Lawnmarket for more than 200 years after Patrick's demise around 1635.

Two Andersons had interesting connections with Captain Cook.

William was a leading surgeon and naturalist who accompanied Cook as surgeon's mate in the Resolution. While speeding over the oceans, his health began to fail and he died of consumption in 1778. An island, sighted the day he died, was named Anderson's Island in his memory. While it can't be identified on modern day maps, there is at least a small town near Brisbane with the proud name Anderson.

The other Anderson was James who was a contributor to the early editions of the

Encyclopaedia Britannica which were published in parts. He claimed that Captain Cook would find 'nothing of importance in the Southern hemisphere except Australia.' His forecast was published seven months before Cook arrived there!

Transport was chosen by another Anderson, Arthur, for his career. So successful was he that he became chairman of the world famous P & O shipping company.

A Shetlander, Arthur Anderson was a ship owner and philosopher. He worked his way up from being a ship broker in Shetland to being boss of the Peninsular Steam Navigation Company. The principle routes were from England to Spain and Portugal. Then in 1840 the company extended its service to Alexandria in Egypt. The name changed to the Peninsular and Orient Steam Navigation Company which became famous as P & O.

It ferried people from Britain to India and the East via the Cape of Good Hope throughout the gracious days of the British

Empire. On those voyages, regular travellers knew to book a cabin on the port side going out and the starboard side on the homeward voyage as this provided more temperate accommodation in the different climate zones they passed through. Their cabin trunks would be marked P.O.S.H. Since it was only first class travellers who had this option of choice, POSH became synonymous with being rich and picky.

INSIGHT POCKET GUIDE

BaRcelona

APA PUBLICATIONS
Part of the Langenscheidt Publishing Group

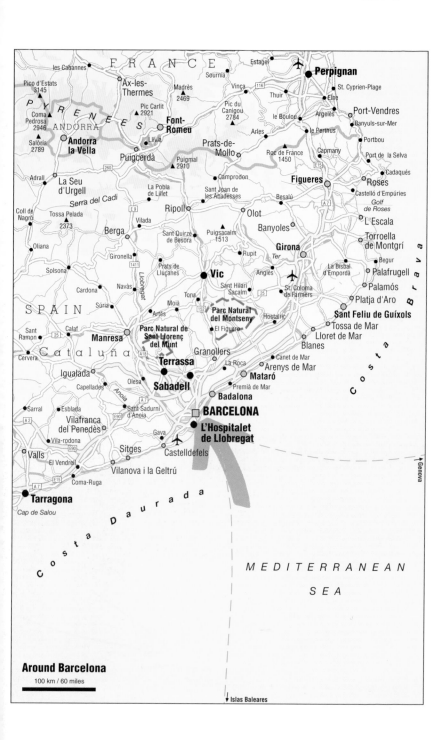

Around Barcelona

100 km / 60 miles

Welcome

This guidebook combines the interests and enthusiasms of two of the world's best-known information providers: Insight Guides, who have set the standard for visual travel guides since 1970, and Discovery Channel, the world's premier source of non-fiction television programming.

Its aim is to help visitors get the most out of Barcelona during a short stay, and to this end Insight Guides' expert on the city, Roger Williams, has created a series of carefully crafted itineraries. The longer tours link the essential sights of La Rambla and the Barri Gòtic, Montjuïc and the waterfront, and the Eixample, with its Modernist architecture and Gaudí's unfinished cathedral; shorter options explore other interesting areas and some lesser-known aspects of the city; and four excursions take in the beach at Sitges, the Holy Mountain of Montserrat, the wine towns of Penedès and the Dalí museums to the north. Supporting the itineraries are sections on history and culture, eating out, shopping, nightlife and practical information.

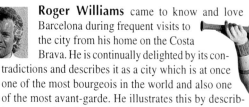

Roger Williams came to know and love Barcelona during frequent visits to the city from his home on the Costa Brava. He is continually delighted by its contradictions and describes it as a city which is at once one of the most bourgeois in the world and also one of the most avant-garde. He illustrates this by describing a scene he witnessed during the rush-hour one morning on La Rambla: 'Walking towards me was a man in a grey jacket, shirt and tie with a briefcase under his arm. His haircut was trim, a little grey at the temples. He was as middle aged and middle class as me, but as he passed I looked down and noticed his short tight blue skirt. Only in Barcelona, I thought.'

EXCURSIONS

Three excursions to destinations within easy reach.

LEISURE ACTIVITIES

CALENDAR OF EVENTS

PRACTICAL INFORMATION

MAPS

INDEX AND CREDITS

Pages 2/3: Casa Battló's sinuous facade
Pages 8/9: the triumphant return of Columbus

BARC

LONA

TANTO MONTA

F.ᵒ Pedro Navia

History & Culture

Barcelona is the capital of the richest region in Spain, with all the amenities you would expect to find in a great metropolis. It has over the centuries been the cradle of both mercantile and industrial Spain. People from other parts of Spain look to it to find work. And *barcelonins* look to the rest of Spain in despair: for every 100 pesetas they pay to Madrid in taxes, they tell you, only 20 pesetas come back in benefits. It is this sense of injustice, combined with a sobriety, a belief in hard work and an unshakeable faith in themselves and their culture that drives a native Catalan *barcelonin* forwards. It may not always be a winning formula, but it is certainly a formidable one, for with it a culture and a language, against enormous odds, have managed to survive very successfully.

The history of the city and of Catalonia, the region of northeast Spain which Madrid has once more allowed a degree of self-control, is a stormy one, with high crests overshadowing deep long troughs. Always its own man, Catalonia has sided with Muslim against Christian, French against Spaniard, anarchist against fascist.

Carthaginians, Romans and Moors

The ancients didn't rate this town site too highly. It had a prominent look-out hill in Montjuïc, and a harbour of sorts, but it was not a greatly fought-over haven. The Iberians had a settlement here and Hamilcar Barca, father of Hannibal, is said to have given it its name as he advanced his Carthaginian armies up from Africa towards his hated Rome.

The retaliating Romans scorned Barcelona, and instead they made their regional capital at Tarragona along the coast. But they built a temple to Jupiter on Montjuïc, and also built the city walls against which the royal palace complex still leans. Their town covered about 12ha (30 acres), centred on Mont Tàber, a high spot where the cathedral now stands; their forum was in the corner of Plaça Sant Jaume, and just inside the entrance to the Centre d'Excursionistes de Catalunya in Carrer Paradís there are a few columns left of a Temple of Augustus.

The Visigoths stepped into the vacuum which was left when the Romans departed. Their chief Athaulf seized the city 'with his best men' and he was later assassinated here, but their architectural legacy is minimal. Nor did the Moors who followed them leave their mark physically, culturally or, more importantly, linguistically, as they did in the rest of Spain. After 85 years they were seen off by the Franks under Charlemagne.

It was Charlemagne, making a buffer state of

Left: painted ladies on an altar urn
Right: Wilfred the Hairy, founder of the House of Barcelona

dependent counties along his southwestern flank, who gave Barcelona its independence, in the 9th century. The first Count of Barcelona to receive a degree of autonomy was Guifré el Pilós (Wilfred the Hairy), who, in a series of campaigns during the 870s, consolidated the counties of northern Catalonia and began the House of Barcelona, a dynasty which continued in an unbroken line for 500 years.

The Boom Begins

The expansion of the cathedral chapters is an indication of the city's early growth – by 1005 there were 17 of them and the canons were fast gaining a reputation for erudition. But Barcelona was not rich in learning alone: the profits of war and the agricultural produce of the surrounding plains made the town materially wealthy, and by the 1070s most of the transactions of the city were made in gold. Some of this money was invested in maritime enterprises: trade was good, a city fleet was established and the word 'Catalan' appeared in documents for the first time. Under Ramón Berenguer III, who reigned from 1082 to 1131, and whose statue stands outside the Royal Chapel in Via Laietana, Provence was acquired by marriage and the Moors were ejected from Tarragona and pushed back beyond the Ebro river.

Over the next two centuries the city rode high. In 1160 a contemporary account records that there were ships from 'Pisa, Genoa, Sicily, Greece, Alexandria and Asia' moored off Barcelona. In the same year Ramón Berenguer IV gave permission for new public baths to be built outside the city wall – today the Carrer dels Banys Nous, the Street of the New Baths. In 1162 Barcelona teamed up with the crown of Aragon, its landlocked inland neighbour, to form the confederation of the count-kings of Catalonia-Aragon.

In 1229 Jaume I, The Conqueror, embarked on a naval expansion which was to swallow up the Balearic islands, Sardinia and Sicily and reach for Greece. At home he knocked down the old city walls and built new ones ten times as long. Up until the 19th century these walls, which contain the Barri Gòtic area, defined the old town. Inland they ran north from Plaça de Catalunya to Passeig Lluís Companys, then down to the sea passing through Ciutadella Park. On the southern side they followed the left bank of the Riera d'en Malla, an intermittent river that ran from the Collserola hills to the sea. This was the *rambla*, the dried-up river bed that became the modern city's exciting thoroughfare.

By the 14th century Catalonia was one of the Mediterranean's most formidable maritime nations and its rule book, the *Consolat de Mar*, governed trade throughout the sea. The 14th century turned the town into a clamorous dustbowl, the Gothic city rose up, riding roughshod over the existing Romanesque: the cathedral, Santa María del Pi, Santa María del Mar, the Royal Palace's Saló de Tinell, the town hall's Saló del Consell de Cent, the trading hall of La Llotja and the great aisles of the Drassanes shipyards, which now house the Maritime Museum.

Left: statue of Ramón Berenguer III outside the Royal Chapel

Even the ravages of the Black Death in the middle of the century did not shatter the city's self confidence or put an end to the building boom.

Unlike much of Spain, Barcelona is not a city of nobles and counts. The tombstones in the cathedral cloisters attest to that. The luminaries buried here are merchants and guildsmen: each one had to buy his slab. The aristocrats of this merchant city favoured the Ribera district in the streets behind the dockside trading hall. The wealthy paid for the building of Santa María del Mar here and they built their mansions and palaces in Carrer de Montcada, several of which now house the Picasso Museum.

The arts were well patronised, and in 1395 annual competitions for poets and troubadors, called the Jocs Florals, were initiated. They were based on a similar event in Toulouse, for Catalonia, which then extended over the Pyrenees into the Roussillon in France, had close links with its neighbour, Languedoc. Their languages were almost the same.

City of Columbus

The year 1992 was not just an important date for Barcelona because of the Olympics. It was also the 500th anniversary of Columbus's discovery of America and the expulsion of the Moors from Spain. It was not in fact until 1493 that Columbus – Cristobal Colón – returned in triumph to Barcelona, to be received by Ferdinand and Isabella in the Saló de Tinell in the Royal Palace. The Genoese navigator, whose statue stands on a great plinth at the foot of La Rambla, did Barcelona little good with his discovery. Seville was the city granted the right to trade with the New World and Barcelona suffered economic decline.

Ferdinand was the end of the Catalonia-Aragon line. When he married Isabella of Castile in 1469 the peninsula became united under one rule. Their daughter married Philip of Austria and thereby introduced the House of Austria to Spain. From that time onwards, Barcelona was to be in constant conflict with the central government, determined to keep its identity, its laws and its customs.

During the Thirty Years' War with France, which began in 1639, Barcelona was less than enthusiastic about supplying arms, men and money to Madrid. As a result mercenary troops were billeted on Catalonia and a viceroy was appointed to keep an eye on the city. Catalonia then declared itself a republic and formed an alliance with the French king, Louis XIII. Not surprisingly, reaction from Madrid was swift. Barcelona was besieged and eventually defeated in 1651. It was allowed to keep its constitution, its *Usatges*, but in the Treaty of the Pyrenees that concluded the war in 1659 all Catalonia north of the Pyrenees was ceded to France.

Above: Ferdinand of Aragon, whose marriage to Isabella of Castile united Spain under one rule

Barcelona could not get away with bucking Madrid again. When Carlos II died without an heir in 1700, a war of succession broke out. The Austrian Habsburg line was favoured by Barcelona, backed by England and Genoa. But the House of Bourbon put up Felipe V who, having been installed on the throne in the Peace of Utrecht in 1713, captured Barcelona after a 13-month siege. The troops entered the city on 11 September, now remembered as La Diada, Catalonia's national day. Revenge was dramatic. All Barcelona's privileges and separate laws were abolished. Books were burned, Catalan banned from official use, the whole of La Ribera district was destroyed and the University, which stood beside the Rambla Estudis, was turned into a barracks.

Industrial Expansion

When the trade ban with the Americas was lifted in 1778, cotton began to arrive, and as the 19th century got underway so did the industrial revolution. The first steamship left the harbour in 1836; 12 years later Spain's first

railway linked Barcelona to the nearby town of Mataró; and in 1842 gas light first illuminated the city. Much of the industry was settled on the north side of the town, in Poble Nou, and huge textile manufacturing centres grew up just inland, at Terrassa and Sabadell. Barcelona itself reached bursting point and the old city wall just had to come down.

In 1859 the plans of the architect Ildefons Cerdà were chosen as a blueprint for the whole of the new city, to be called the Eixample (Extension), spreading inland from the Plaça de Catalunya. Keeping to a grid system, the blocks of houses lined the wide boulevards. The biggest, the Gran Via de les Corts Catalanes, cuts the city in half and today allows a driver to go straight through, south to north, without turning left or right. Many of the city's monasteries were dissolved and pulled down, which is how the Liceu theatre and the Palau de la Música Catalana found their sites.

The new building gave great scope for architects and designers. Their patrons were industrialists such as Eusebi Güell and the emerging bourgeoisie, and a new spirit of national identity began to take a grip. It was a rebirth, the Renaixença, and it was not confined to any one class or political set. The Jocs Florals were revived and the Catalan language, only handed down orally since the Bourbons' decree, was written and published once more. This cultural rediscovery burst on to the world stage in 1887 when it

Above: a painting by Ramón Casas, the most representative of the Modernista artists who flourished at the end of the 19th century

was suddenly decided to hold a Universal Exhibition in Ciutadella Park the following year. The exhibition triggered the Modernisme movement, Barcelona's version of art nouveau.

Increasing prosperity encouraged Barcelona to look down on Madrid even more. This prosperity was not all of its own making: its products were sold in the protected markets of Spain's American colonies, and there was an outcry in Barcelona when these colonies were lost at the end of the 19th century. Then, in 1909, the city excelled itself in 'Tragic Week'. In response to a national call-up of reserves to fight in Morocco, which *barcelonins* wanted nothing to do with, a mob took to the streets and destroyed 70 buildings of religious orders, killing 116 people and injuring 300.

Anarchy and Civil War

Catalanism was now at the centre of the political agenda and in 1914 the Mancomunitat, a local Catalan council, was established, only to be removed again in the 1923 coup by the city's military governor, Primo de Rivera, whose dictatorship lasted seven years. Elections in 1931 brought the veteran Catalan campaigner Francesc Macià to power. He declared Catalonia a republic, but it only lasted three days. Three years later his successor Lluís Companys did it again. This time Madrid sent in the army and Companys was jailed. But in 1936 the popular front was elected in Madrid and he was released. Soon afterwards, on 18 July, General Franco led the Nationalist rebellion, and the Spanish Civil War had begun.

The army in Barcelona, under General Goded, declared for Franco and marched on the city from the Bruc barracks near Pedralbes. After heavy fighting, Goded was defeated by the civil authorities and executed. Thereafter Catalonia was the staunchest of the Republican areas. But when Franco's army arrived in the city, Barcelona surrendered without a shot. Tens of thousands fled over the Pyrenees into exile, tens of thousands more were executed in reprisals. Once again the Catalan language was banned.

Above: a naval battle depicted in a painting in the Maritime Museum

The years following the Civil War were extremely hard. The rest of Europe turned its back on Madrid, and Madrid turned its back on Barcelona. But this is a region of workers who will not be kept down. The 1960s saw an economic boom and between 1960 and 1975 more than two million Spaniards came to work in the city.

A New Renaissance

On Franco's death in 1975 there was free champagne in the streets. Juan Carlos, Alfons XIII's grandson, returned to the throne and wisely some degree of autonomy was restored to Catalonia and other regions. In 1980, the conservative Jordi Pujol was elected president of Catalonia and promoted his 'country' around the world, attracting investors from America to Japan. In the latest elections (1999), despite strong opposition from the charismatic former mayor, socialist Pasqual Maragall, he was again re-elected, an indication of support from the Catalan heartland rather than Barcelona.

Barcelona had begun another Renaixença, another rebirth. The Catalan language is now taught in all schools, with Castilian (Spanish) as a second language. Two native Catalans would not dream of talking to one another in any other language. Theatre is in Catalan, and heroes from Barcelona's history are commemorated in newly revised street names. The media and arts are also all dominated by Catalan.

The 1992 Olympics gave impetus to this rebirth. Suddenly there was money to invest in the city's infrastructure, to renovate old buildings and to build new roads. This is post-industrial Barcelona, a city that still attracts investment and huge numbers of workers, a city that still likes to think of itself as avant-garde and different from the rest of Spain.

The Olympic programme has had a lasting effect: when the cheering stopped, people found themselves in a new city with its axis tilted to the north. The Olympic Village left it with a proper waterfront after decades of turning its back on the sea, and the industrial area of Poble Nou has become fashionable. There is a new airport, new culture palaces such as the museum of contemporary art, the national theatre, the auditorium, and more to come. Barcelona has entered the 21st century with confidence but will continue to look over its shoulder to its even more glorious past.

HISTORY HIGHLIGHTS

3000BC Neolithic tombs constructed beneath Carrer Montcada.

700 Iberian settlement established on Montjuïc.

Circa 230 Barcelona is founded by Hamil Barca, Carthaginian leader and father of Hannibal, whose war with Rome provokes the Romans to land in Spain, at Empúries, north of Barcelona.

200BC–AD410 Under Roman occupation Barcelona is a relatively small settlement, based around Mont Tàber near the site of the present cathedral. The Romans make their main base at Tarragona, to the south.

AD 412 Visigoths arrive, making Barcelona their capital from 531–48.

717 Moors occupy the city, but leave little evidence of their rule.

801 Franks, under Charlemagne, eject the Moors and set up the Spanish March, a buffer state.

878 Wilfred the Hairy (Guifré el Pilós), Count of Barcelona, consolidates the eastern Pyrenees and is given autonomy by the Franks. Thus begins 500-year family rule of the region.

1060 The Catalan constitution, called the Usatges, is drawn up.

1162 The Counts of Barcelona join a confederation with neighbouring kingdom of Aragon, and become kings in their own right.

1213 Jaume I (The Conqueror) begins naval expansion. The Catalan Consolat de Mar establishes trading practices throughout the Mediterranean.

1395 Jocs Florals, troubadors' Olympics, are introduced. This is the period of the flowering of Catalan culture.

1479 Ferdinand of Catalonia-Aragon marries Isabella of Castile, thus uniting Spain.

1493 Columbus returns from the New World, but Catalonia is barred from trading with the Americas, a privilege which is given to Seville. Economic decline soon follows.

1640–52 Revolt of the harvesters, *els segadors*.

1714 Barcelona is sacked by Bourbon king Felipe V. The University is closed, books burned, the Catalan language banned and La Ribera district of the city is destroyed.

1808–14 The French occupy Barcelona during the Peninsula War. Montserrat is sacked.

1835 Monasteries dissolved and their properties confiscated.

1848 The first Spanish railway built between Barcelona and Mataró

1859 Revival of Jocs Florals, cornerstone of the Renaixença. Cerdà plans the rebuilding of Barcelona, in what is now the Eixample.

1888 Universal Exhibition is held in Ciutadella Park.

1901–9 Years of anarchism and strikes culminate in the Tragic Week when 70 religious institutions are razed.

1929 International Exhibition takes place in Montjuïc.

1931 Macià declares an independent Catalonia, which only lasts a few days.

1936 Spanish Civil War. The Republican government retreats from Madrid to Valencia, then to Barcelona, but is finally defeated by insurgent Nationalists led by General Franco.

1939 Franco's dictatorship begins. The Catalan language is banned from official use.

1975 Death of Franco. The Bourbon line is restored with King Juan Carlos I.

1978 Under a new constitution, semi-autonomy is granted to Catalonia.

1992 Olympic Games held in Barcelona.

1990s Barcelona internationally recognised for its urban regeneration.

2000 Barcelona greets the millennium with yet more exciting development.

Left: the fiery arrow that ignited the Olympic torch in 1992

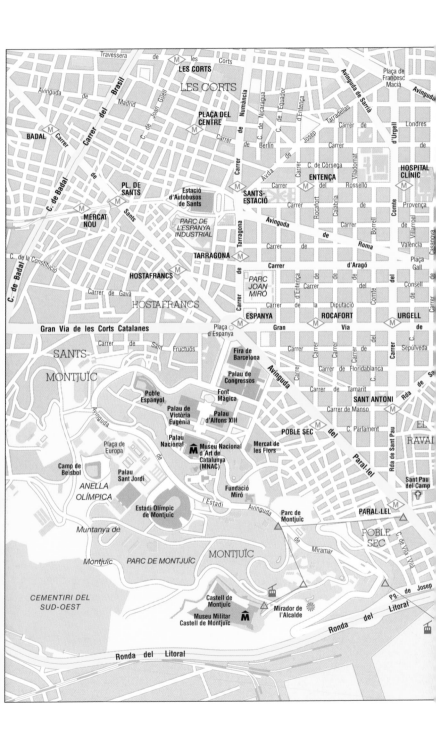

Barcelona
500 m / 550 yds

City Itineraries

arcelona has no need of your car – it has more than enough of its own. It also has inexpensive and frequently used taxis, buses and a metro and train system that is simplicity itself: a single-fare ticket will take you to any part of the central network and beyond; a book of 10 tickets, for the price of slightly less than six, will keep you going for hours on both trains and buses. Transport is often a delight: cable cars and funiculars take you to the city's mountains, boat trips take you round the bay and there are even open-air escalators.

For the visitor, the city is not hard to get around and much of it can be conquered on foot. Look at the map: back from the port is the old town, the Barri Gòtic, centred on the cathedral. It has not had to suffer the modern indignity of pedestrianisation, because many of its lanes were built for nothing wider than a horse and cart in the first place. One-way signs for horse-drawn traffic are still pinned to solid stone walls.

Beside these warrens runs the famous Rambla, which leads from the old port and waterfront up to the Plaça de Catalunya, the heart of the city. From here the broad, chic shopping streets, Rambla de Catalunya and Passeig de Gràcia, run inland through the 19th-century new town, the Eixample, across the Diagonal and the Gran Via, the widest of the city's thoroughfares.

A little farther afield lie the Sagrada Família, Antoni Gaudí's great unfinished masterpiece, the Gothic monastery of Pedralbes, and the Park Güell, originally the property of Gaudí's patron, Eusebi Güell, and full of wonderfully decorative touches. There are plenty of open spaces if you need to relax, from the Parc de la Ciutadella, which also encompasses a zoo and several museums, to the Parc de Montjuïc, where the the 1992 Olympic buildings were constructed. And, of course, there's Tibidabo, the summit of the Collserola hills, where there are splendid views of the city, peaceful walks, a great amusement park and the church of the Sagrat Cor.

Barcelona's port is a fascinating place to wander, and your exploration may lead you on to Barceloneta and the beaches, a once-industrial area that was regenerated for the Olympic Games and is now a great spot to eat or swim.

Dip and Delve

When the feet get tired there are always tempting cafés that need checking out. Don't be afraid to ignore your map sometimes and go slightly off the beaten track. Dive down beckoning alleys or carry on around corners which entice you with their markets, mansions or shop windows, for there is no better city in which to become lost.

Left: the towers of Gaudí's Sagrada Família
Right: Tibidabo tram

1. LA RAMBLA *(see map, p23)*

If you only have a day to spare, this is the itinerary for you. From the Plaça de Catalunya down La Rambla to the Boqueria market. Into the Gothic quarter to the town hall and cathedral. From the Picasso Museum via the Santa María church to the seafront. Finally to the city's liveliest square, Plaça Reial.

Opened in 1927, the **Plaça de Catalunya** is the meeting point of the old and new cities. It is also a space for demonstrations and rock concerts. At the metro exit in the southern corner, near the statue commemorating Francesc Macià, is the **Café Zurich**, a city institution that has been rebuilt in the commercial centre, El Triangle. The world passes by its pavement tables, shoe-shiners operate, lottery tickets are sold: a good place for a coffee before starting out.

From here the famous **Rambla** begins, a 1.5-km (1-mile) long avenue of colourful bird, flower and news stands spread out beneath the shade of plane trees alongside café tables; musicians, mime artists, tango dancers, fire eaters, fortune tellers and other entertainers ensure constant diversion at all hours of the day and night. The Rambla is in fact made up of five consecutive *rambles*: the Canaletes, Estudis, Sant Josep, Caputxins and Santa Mònica, the last three taking their names from the convents that lined the southwest (right-hand) side of the street. On the left-hand side was the medieval city's perimeter wall.

At the top of La Rambla is the cast-iron Canaletes drinking fountain, a meeting place for Barça football fans. Taste these waters, it is said, and you will come back to the city again. Further down on the right at No 115 is the **Poliorama** theatre. This was built as the Royal Acad-

Above: the Rambla is the city's favourite meeting place
Left: street entertainers keep the crowds amused

emy of Sciences and Arts and on its facade is the city's first clock, erected in 1888 and inscribed 'Hora Official' ('Official Time').

Mare de Déu de Betlem, a recently renovated 17th-century baroque church, is the next notable building on the right. Opposite, on the corner of Carrer Portaferrissa, is the colonnade of the bookshop of the Generalitat (the Catalan autonomous government).

The shop occupies part of the ground floor of the **Palau Moja**. Look up through the first-floor windows to see the Grand Salon's fine baroque murals by Francesc Pla (1743–92); the Salon is sometimes used for exhibitions. Another exhibition site is the nearby **Palau de la Virreina**, built by Spain's viceroy to Peru, whose young widow occupied it on its completion in 1777. It also houses a municipal cultural information centre, box office and a stylish souvenir shop with the best of Barcelona design.

La Boqueria, more properly the Mercat Sant Josep, is just past the mansion on the right. This is the market where the top restaurateurs do their early-morning shopping and it is a palace of food not to be passed by. Built like a great art nouveau railway station, it offers, within a few strides, all the flavours and aromas of Catalonia's countryside and cuisine. Look out for *fungi* in season, for brightly coloured vegetables and fruit, assortments of olives, cheeses and nuts, for butchers' stalls selling parts of animals you would rather not eat and, of course, seafood glistening in ice.

Beyond the market on the corner of Carrer Petxina is an attractive mosaic-fronted shop, the **Antigua Casa Figueras**, owned by the famous Barcelona chocolate maker, Antoni Escribá. Try 100 grams of his chocolate cats. A little further down on the left, on the corner of Carrer Cardenal Casañas, is **Casa Bruno Quadras**, an orientally inspired building with a green dragon, designed for an umbrella shop in 1891. Beyond it the road is set slightly back in the Pla de la Boqueria, which served as a place of execution during the 14th century. In the middle of the Rambla is a fading pavement mosaic by Joan Miró and on the far side is the city's opera house, the **Gran Teatre del Liceu**, rebuilt and enlarged since it was almost entirely destroyed in a fire in 1994.

The Barri Gòtic

It is time to leave the Rambla and dive into the Barri Gòtic, the Gothic quarter, which spreads its narrow alleys and solid walls out around the cathedral, palace and town hall. From the Pla de la Boqueria, head down the Carrer Boqueria, past Obach's hat shop into the Carrer del Call. The lane emerges into daylight at the Plaça Sant Jaume, the administrative

heart of the city. The left side of the square is occupied by the elegant **Palau de la Generalitat**, from which Catalonia is governed. Opposite is the **Casa de la Ciutat**, Barcelona's town hall. It is sometimes possible to visit the town hall: enquire at the entrance, which is flanked by the figures of the saintly King Jaume I and Joan Fiveller, a 15th-century councillor who established city freedoms. The building's two most notable rooms are the 14th-century Saló del Consell de Cent, where concerts are sometimes held, and the Saló de les Cròniques where, in 1928, Josep María Sert painted scenes from the 14th-century Catalan expedition to Byzantium.

The Generalitat on the opposite side of the square is a Gothic building with Renaissance additions to its facade. One of the few occasions when it is

open to the public is 23 April, St George's Day. Since George (Sant Jordi) is the patron saint of Catalonia, this day calls for celebration and the square and surrounding streets are filled with stalls selling books and roses. A further reason for commemoration is that it is the anniversary of the death of Miguel de Cervantes (1547–1616) and has been declared World Book Day. The Generalitat's 15th-century St George's Chapel and first-floor Patí dels Tarongers (Orange Tree Patio) are among its principal architectural treasures.

The lane leading up the right-hand side of the Generalitat is the Carrer del Bisbe. On the right is the 14th-century **Casa dels Canonges** (Canons' House), now Generalitat offices. An overhead neo-Gothic bridge, based on the Bridge of Sighs in Venice, links the two buildings. Before the end of this street a portal on the right leads to the **cathedral cloisters**. Enclosed by a 15th-century iron railing, its cool atmosphere is emphasised by the mossy **Font de les Oques**, a fountain which takes its name from the 13 geese which live in the cloisters.

From the cloister, enter the **Cathedral of Santa Eulàlia** (8am–1.30pm, 4–7.30pm, entrance fee), begun in 1298 under Jaume II and completed in 1417. It has three naves and a central choir. Below the altar is the crypt of Santa Eulàlia. Her remains were placed here 1,000 years after she was martyred in the Roman purges of Dacian, and her alabaster tomb, behind the altar, was carved in 1327. Of the 29 side chapels the most interesting is that of Sant Salvador, with a *Transfiguration* (1442) by Bernat Martorell.

Outside the main door is the spacious Pla de la Seu, which allows a full view of the main north front of the cathedral, completed in the late 19th century. To the west, on Carrer Santa Llúcia, is the 15th-century **Casa de l'Ardiaca** (Archdeacon's House), built on Roman ruins. A letterbox decorated with swallows and a tortoise was added as part of later remodelling in

Above: a service in the cathedral. **Above Right:** the cathedral's Gothic doorway.
Bottom Right: walkers from all walks of life

1908 by Domènech i Montaner. Don't miss its courtyard, where a palm tree rises above an elegant fountain. The street running down the opposite side of the cathedral, is the Carrer dels Comtes which leads to the **Plaça del Rei**, home of the count-kings of Catalonia-Aragon. *(To explore this area in detail, see The Royal and Roman Town, page 35.)*

Exit down Carrer Veguer to **Baixada Llibreteria** or **Jaume I** to find lunch. A drink at the quaint Mesón del Café (closed Sunday) may be supplemented with pastries from nearby shops, for example a *tartaleta de music* (mixed nut tartlet) or *empanada catalana*, a pie filled with tuna and olives. Try *tapes* at one of the bars, or tortillas at the Haití.

Palaces and Picasso

The **Museu Picasso** (10am–8pm, Sun 10am–3pm, closed Mon, entrance fee) is 10 minutes' walk away. Continue along Baixada Llibreteria, noting the candle sellers at No 7: Pauli Subirà is the city's oldest shop and dates from 1761. Cross the busy Via Laietana and continue along the Carrer de la Princesa. The third turning on the right is **Carrer Montcada**, built by the city's aristocrats from the 12th to the 14th century. The Palau Berenguer d'Aguilar at No 15 and four neighbouring palaces house the Museu Picasso and should be visited almost as much for their splendid interiors as for the 3,000 works of art, mainly from the Spanish artist's early life.

Continue down Carrer Montcada to Passeig del Born. This area, around the old **Mercat del Born**, a late 19th-century wrought-iron covered market being remodelled to house the largest library in the city, is becoming an increasingly fashionable artists' haunt and a popular night spot. On the right a door leads into **Santa María del Mar** (9.30am–1.30pm, 4.30–8pm,

entrance fee), the city's best-loved church. Built in the middle of the 14th century by the maritime enterprises that brought wealth and excitement to this part of town, its lofty nave reaches Catalan-Gothic heights. Pleasingly simple, its octagonal pillars are exceptionally far apart until they close ranks around the altar to form an ambulatory. Stand by the main door for a full sense of the space, as light from the 15th-century rose window warms even the ceiling's grey cobbles.

Exit through the main door into the Plaça Santa María and take the street in the far left corner, Carrer Canvis Vells, which leads to the Carrer Consolat del Mar and the **Llotja**, the former stock exchange. Picasso's father taught at the art school which occupied the upper part of the building, and Picasso and Miró were both students there. Cross back over the Via Laietana and then over the Passeig de Colom past Roy Lichtenstein's *Cap de Barcelona*.

On the Waterfront

Back on the waterfront wander along the palm-studded **Moll de la Fusta**, past the bars which come to life at night, to the **Monument a Colom** (Columbus Monument). *(See Itinerary 8, page 44 for a guided walk around the port.* Now cross back over to La Rambla and take the fourth turning on the left,

Carrer Nou de la Rambla. Just down on the left, at Nos 3–5, is **Palau Güell** (guided tours Mon–Fri 10am–2pm, 4–6.30pm), Count Eusebi Güell's townhouse. Outwardly gloomy but full of hidden treasures, it was designed by Gaudí and built between 1885 and 1890, but the Güell family only lived in it for a couple of years.

On the opposite side of La Rambla is the Plaça Reial, one of the city's liveliest squares. Cafés fill its colonnades, drug pedlars lurk on its fringes, police prowl and backpackers sleep off their overnight journeys. This is an entertaining place for *tapes* or an evening meal before strolling back up the increasingly animated Rambla to the Plaça de Catalunya.

Above: looking down on Plaça Reial
Left: inside Santa María del Mar

2. MONTJUÏC *(see map, p28)*

Barcelona's southern hill is a place of culture, leisure and sport. This route starts at the Plaça d'Espanya, leads past the Palau Nacional, via the Mercat de les Flors and Teatre Grec, to the Fundació Miró, then takes a cable car to Castell de Montjuïc. The return route includes the Olympic buildings, the Museu Nacional d'Art de Catalunya and Poble Espanyol.

The buildings which were at the centre of the 1992 Olympic Games are the latest of many attractions in Barcelona's showground. Scattered over the northern side of 213-m (700-ft) Montjuïc hill are remnants of the last great hullabaloo, the International Exhibition of 1929.

The best way to approach Montjuïc is from the **Plaça d'Espanya**, which is served by Metro lines 1 and 3. This allows you to walk up through the Venetian pillars which flagged the triumphant approach to the 1929 exhibition, along Avinguda de la Reina María Cristina and past the trade fair halls towards the imposing, if not particularly beautiful, Palau Nacional. The Palau can be reached by escalators, but we will go by a more circuitous route.

At the top of the avenue is the **Font Màgica** (Magic Fountain), designed by Carles Buïgas in 1929. Rising to 50m (164ft) and lit by coloured lights, it offers a grand free show (Jun–Sep, Thur–Sun 8pm–midnight). Turn left at the steps in front of the fountain along Avinguda de Rius i Taulet, first right up Carrer Guardia Urbana, second left around the Palau Municipal d'Esports, along Carrer Segons Jocs Mediterranis and right into Carrer de Lleida. This may sound complicated but it is only following the bottom of the rising hill.

Among a collection of left-over exhibition buildings beside Carrer de Lleida is the **Mercat de les Flors**, which is currently being remodelled in an ambitious project to become the Ciutat del Teatre (Theatre City), a complex of theatres which will accommodate every possible stage production by the year 2004.

Archaeology and Miró

Continue up to the **Museu d'Arqueologia** in Passeig Santa Madrona (9.30am–7pm, Sun 10am–2.30pm, closed Mon; entrance fee). Built for the 1929 exhibition as the Palace of Graphic Arts, it now houses finds from the city and the Graeco-Roman trading post at Empúries on the Costa Brava. Opposite the museum is a public garden leading to the open-air **Teatre Grec** . Another exhibition remnant, it is still used for plays and concerts in the summer Grec festival. Behind is the angular Miró gallery. Climb the steps at the side of the theatre to reach it.

Right: the Palau Nacional, which houses the Museu Nacional d'Art de Catalunya

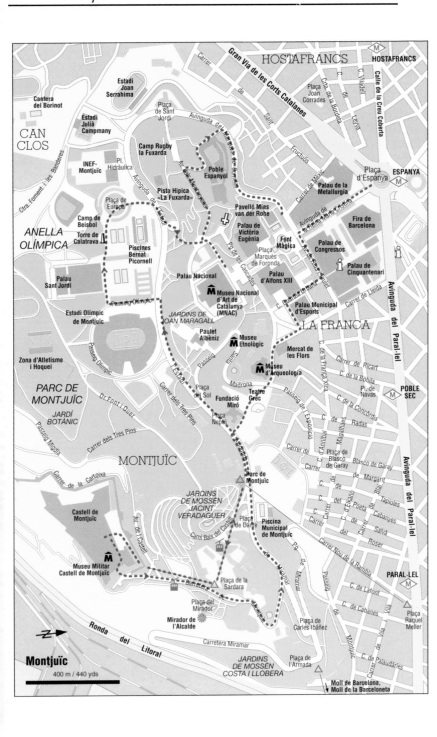

Montjuïc

400 m / 440 yds

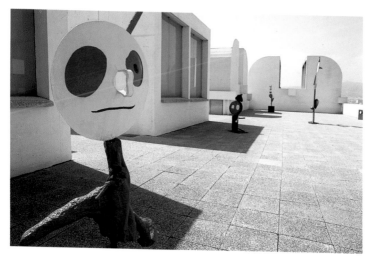

The **Fundació Joan Miró** (10am–7pm, Thur 10am–9.30pm, Sun 10am–2.30pm, closed Mon; entrance fee), one of the finest exhibition venues in Europe, is a monument to two men: the painter Joan Miró (1893–1983) and the architect Josep Lluís Sert (1902–83). They were both from Barcelona and were friends, but lived most of their lives in exile from the Franco regime, Miró in Paris then Mallorca, Sert at Harvard where he succeeded his mentor, Walter Gropius, as head of the faculty of architecture. Flooded with light, the gallery, which opened in 1975, houses one of the largest collections of Miró's work in the world, including his bright sculptures out on the roof. Concerts are held here regularly, and there's a pleasant restaurant.

View from the Top

From the gallery, continue walking up Avinguda de Miramar for a few minutes until the Teleferic station appears. A ride on one of these **cable cars** gives wonderful birds'-eye views of the city. They run all the way to the castle at the top, coming to a halt by a café with a long terrace which looks out over the city and inland to Tibidabo.

Castell de Montjuïc at the top was built in 1640 during the Harvesters' Revolt and redesigned during the reign of Felipe V. In 1939, at the end of the civil war, it was used as a prison and execution ground. Today it houses a **Museu Militar** (9.30am–7.30pm, closed Mon; entrance fee). Exhibits include arms and uniforms, plus models of other castles in the region. Its battlements provide an impressive 360-degree panorama, particularly of the port

Return via cable car or walk down Carreterra de Montjuïc past the former amusement park to the Plaça del Mirador. Keep going past the Miró Foundation and the buildings of the **Anella Olímpica** (Olympic Ring) soon appear on the left. This elegant and spacious showcase includes the remodelled 1929 stadium (with a permanent exhibition of the

Above: the Fundació Joan Miró
Right: riding the cable car

1992 event in the Galeria Olímpica by the south gate, 10am–2pm, 4–8pm, Sun 10am–2pm); Japanese architect Arata Isozaki's Palau Sant Jordi, an ultra-modern indoor sports stadium; Ricardo Bofill's neoclassical sports college; and the stunning 188-m (616-ft) Torre de Calatrava communication tower, as well as fine views over the south of the city.

Cross over Avinguda de l'Estadi, and head to the **Palau Nacional**, the huge palace which dominates the approach to Montjuïc. Home to the **Museu Nacional d'Art de Catalunya** (10am–7pm, Thur 10am–9pm, Sun 10am–2.30pm, closed Mon; entrance fee), it has the finest collection of Romanesque art in the world. The most striking of its 70 rooms are those containing wall paintings peeled off the apses of remote Pyrenean churches in the early 20th century, transported here by mule train and restored. There is a good collection of Gothic art and a smaller one of Renaissance and baroque works.

Spanish Village

Outside the Palau Nacional turn left and follow Avinguda dels Montanyans down to the **Poble Espanyol** or Spanish Village (9am till late; fee includes a plan of the village). This concoction of buildings, covering 2ha (5 acres) represents architecture from all over Spain, from Moorish Andalusia to the rugged Basque country. It was designed for the 1929 exhibition by Francesc Fulguera and Ramón Raventós with the help of artists such as Maurice Utrillo. Since then it has become a leisure centre with craft shops, restaurants, squares, cafés and live entertainment.

There are also two museums in the village, the Museu d'Arts, Indústries i Tradicions Populars, which concentrates on arts and crafts, and the Museu de les Arts Gràfiques, with exhibits on graphic design. The village really does seem to have something for everyone, including children and teenagers.

Turn right outside the village, and head down Avinguda del Marquès de Comillas. The **Pavelló Mies van der Rohe** (10am–8pm, Sat–Sun 11am–7pm; entrance fee) is on the right. It was built by the Bauhaus director as the German pavilion for the 1929 exhibition, later demolished, and rebuilt in 1986 to celebrate the centenary of his birth. Its glass and marble planes and unruffled pool are impressive, even after all these years.

Opposite the pavilion is the impressive Modernista factory, the **Casa Ramona**, built in 1911 by architect Josep Puig i Cadafalch and now converted into a cultural centre.

Above: the Poble Espanyol has something for all age groups
Right: the entrance hall at Casa Lleó Morera

3. GAUDÍ AND THE DESIGNER CITY *(see map, p33)*

Up the Passeig de Gràcia into the Eixample to see the fine Modernista buildings. The itinerary includes the best designer shops, a visit to the Fundació Tàpies, and ends up at the Sagrada Família and Park Güell.

Anyone who knows Barcelona will know the name of Antoni Gaudí. He made his mark on the city as Wren did on London or Eiffel on Paris. This tour of his main works takes in other examples of Modernista architecture designed by his contemporaries. It also shows the best of modern design in a city which likes to think itself stylish, and it includes the monographic museum, to Barcelona's greatest living artist.

Most of the city's Modernista work is in the **Eixample** (Extension), the new part of town laid out in an 1860 grid plan by Ildefons Cerdà i Sunyer, which offered great opportunity for a newly rich bourgeoisie to build showy homes. The Rambla de Catalunya and the Passeig de Gràcia are its principle shopping streets, running from the top corners of the Plaça de Catalunya.

Start at the Passeig de Gràcia Metro, on lines 2, 3 and 4. Unmissable on the western side of this main shopping thoroughfare, between Carrer d'Aragó and Carrer del Consell de Cent at Nos 35–43, is a trilogy of Catalan Modernista works. On the southern corner of the block is the **Casa Lleó Morera**. Three houses up is **Casa Amatller**, now the centre for the Modernisme Route, an option for visiting key buildings normally closed to the public, by purchasing a multi-ticket. Next to it is Gaudí's **Casa Batlló**, the facade covered in blue-green ceramic work, and the windows sensuously curved.

In Catalan *mansana* means both apple and block. These three buildings are known as the 'Mansana de la Discordia', the Block of Discord, each of them striking in different ways. The architect of Casa Lleó Morera was Lluís Domènech i Montaner (1850–1923: for his masterpiece, the Palau de la Música Catalana, *see Itinerary 6, page 40*). He was the mentor of Josep Puig i Cadafalch (1867–1957), designer of the neighbouring Dutch-gabled Casa Amatller. Both were polymaths, parliamentarians, literary luminaries and leading figures of the Renaixença, the Catalan Renaissance begun in the 19th century.

By contrast Antoni Gaudí i Cornet (1852–1926) was a single-minded ar-

chitect, and though as fiercely Catalan as the others he was a private person, a reactionary with deep religious convictions who became a recluse in later life. At the age of 74 he was run down by a tram and, mistaken for a tramp, he was taken to the old hospital in El Raval where he died two days later.

After the Block of Discord, turn left into Carrer d'Aragó. At No 255, on the north side, crowned with a twisted metal sculpture called 'Cloud and Chair', is the **Fundació Tàpies** (11am–8pm, closed Mon). It houses a large collection of Tàpies' own work and regularly holds visiting exhibitions.

Antoni Tàpies, born in Barcelona in 1923, was a friend of Miró and became identified with a separate Catalan culture through his work, which is abstract and uncompromising. His paintings do not always work well in isolation and it is through this museum that he is able to give a clearer account of himself, for he is a painter of integrity and intelligence. The foundation is part gallery and part study centre, and visitors may find themselves walking on works of art laid out across the floor. Designed by Lluís Domènech i Montaner as an office for his brother's publishing company, it was built in 1880 and was the first domestic construction in the city to employ an iron frame.

From La Pedrera to the Sagrada Família

Return down Aragó to the wide, tree-lined Passeig de Gràcia, cross the road and walk up to No 92 on the corner of Carrer de Provença, where Casa Milà, often called **La Pedrera** is situated. Its name means the Stone Quarry, and was inspired by its rippling grey stone facade. This is Gaudí's most prominent private building, an eight-storey apartment block devoid of straight lines, set around two inner courtyards. Gaudí put the city's first underground carriage park in the basement and sculpted a roof of evil-looking chimneys which have gained the name *espantabruixes*, witch-scarers. Begun in 1901, this was an extremely controversial project. After years of being allowed to fall into decay it was rescued when UNESCO declared it a building of world interest and the Caixa de Catalunya foundation undertook its restoration. One apartment, decorated as it was in 1908, can be visited, along with the roof and an exhibition area (daily 10am–8pm; entrance fee).

Just beyond La Pedrera, at No 96, is **Vinçon**, the leading designer store for household goods. There is a great deal to look at, from stylish stationery to furniture and fabrics, and there are often exhibitions. Go upstairs to appreciate the building fully. This was once the home of the artist Ramón Casas

Above: the spooky chimneys of La Pedrera, with the Sagrada Família in the background

(1866–1932), some of whose work can be seen in the Museu d'Art Modern *(see Itinerary 9, page 46).*

At Plaça Rei Joan Carles I, turn down Avinguda Diagonal. On the right, at No 373, is the **Palau Baró de Quadras** by Puig i Cadafalch (1904). This is now the **Museu de la Música** (10am–2pm, Wed until 8pm, closed Mon; entrance fee), occupying three floors of its delightful interior, and with one of the most important guitar collections in the world. Puig i Cadafalch's **Casa de les Punxes** (House of the Spikes), officially called Casa Terrades, is a neo-Gothic apartment building on the opposite side of the avenue two blocks further down. You can't go inside, but the exterior is impressive.

Turn right down Carrer de Roger de Llúria and at the corner of Carrer de Mallorca are the **Palau Casades** on the north side and on the south side **Palau Montaner** which has attractively tiled eaves. It was designed by Domènech i Montaner, again for his brother but this time as a private home and the whole family lived here from 1893 until 1939.

Domènech i Montaner also built **Casa Thomas** at Carrer de Mallorca 291–3, a few yards down on the left. This is now occupied by **b.d. Ediciones de Diseño**, the city's most prestigious design organisation. Don't be intimidated by the office look of its entrance. Walk straight in to admire its exquisite products, from beautiful Fortuny lampshades and Gaudí furniture to the very best in modern work by local designers such as Oscar Tusquets, and others from a number of different countries. The showrooms are set out on two floors with a further room at the back.

After Gaudí had completed his last commission – Casa Milà – in 1910, he devoted his remaining 16 years to the Expiatory Temple of the Holy Family, the **Sagrada Família** (Apr–Aug, daily 9am–8pm; Mar, Sep–Oct, 9am–7pm; Nov–Feb, 9am–6pm; entrance fee). To reach the building, which is 10 minutes' walk from b.d., continue along Carrer de Mallorca and cross

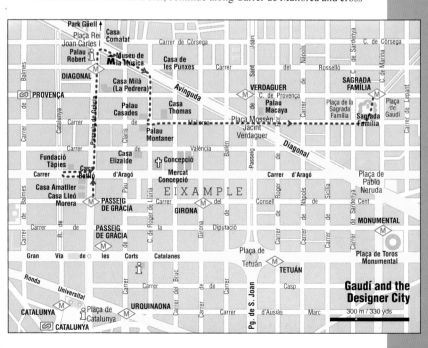

the Diagonal. As you do so, you will see the **Casa Macaya**, the cultural centre of the Caixa de Catalunya foundation. It hosts some good temporary exhibitions and concerts. The graceful arches of the patio and the decorated staircase are well worth a look as you pass.

Gaudí completed the temple's crypt (now the museum), where he is buried, and the famous eastern Nativity facade. This has three doorways to Faith, Hope and Charity, and aspires to four coloured, tentacled towers, one of which has an internal lift to take vertigo-free visitors skywards, though they must descend by an even more nerve-wracking spiral staircase.

Continuing work has involved a local sculptor, Josep María Subirachs, and a Japanese one, Etsuro Soto. The museum shows how Gaudí envisaged the finished temple, and also shows that his ideas often changed. A scale model reveals how the pillars in the nave, which has served as a builder's yard, will be like an avenue of trees in an enchanted wood.

At 110m (360ft) in length, the Sagrada Família will eventually be 27m (87ft) longer than the city's cathedral and nearly twice the height, with a main tower rising to 198m (650ft), half as high again as those that are already there. Gaudí spent his last 10 dedicated and unpaid years in a hut on the site. He didn't have much time for his own comforts, but a glimpse of his own surroundings can be had in the house that he lived in at Park Güell.

Park Güell

Time to stop walking now and take a taxi, or else take Metro Line 5 from the Sagrada Família back to Diagonal and change there on to the northbound Line 3, travelling two stops to Lesseps. From the station either take an eastbound 24 bus to **Park Güell**, or turn left off Travessera de Dalt up Avinguda Santuari de Sant Josep de la Muntanya: the park lies 15 minutes' walk away at the top of this street. This space is always popular. Children play around its coloured animals and chase between the pillars that support the wavy, tile-mosaic parapet from where there is a grand view out over the city. This long, curving bench, perhaps the most photographed aspect of the park, was the work not of Gaudí but of his assistant, Josep Jujol i Gibert.

The park was originally owned by Gaudí's patron, the industrialist Eusebi Güell who had wanted to create a garden city of houses – hence the English spelling of Park. The space beneath the balcony was intended to be a market. Gaudí bought the home of architect Francesc Berenguer, a few hundred metres to the right of the entrance, and this is now the **Casa Museu Gaudí** (May– Sep, 10am–8pm, Mar, Apr–Oct, 10am– 7pm, Nov–Feb, 10am–6pm; entrance fee). It contains assorted drawings and projects by Gaudí, but there is little sign of his soul, which is so evident in his unfinished cathedral.

Above: sun-burst design in Park Güell
Left: the spires remain unfinished

4. THE ROYAL AND ROMAN TOWN *(see map, p36)*

This tour takes a more detailed look at the historic and royal Barri Gòtic quarter, starting at the Plaça Nova.

The **Plaça Nova** is at the west end of Avinguda Catedral, the large open space that lies in front of the cathedral (Metro to Liceu, Line 3, or Jaume I, Line 4). From here the Roman wall that encircled the 4th-century city begins its surviving 1.5-km (1-mile) stretch. It is easily identified by its colossal stones, the largest of which is 3.5m (12ft) thick and 9.5m (30ft) high. The end of the wall, in Plaça Nova, is marked by the twin round towers of the **Portal del Bisbe**, the Roman city's north gate, and is incorporated into the adjacent Casa de l'Ardiaca (Archdeacon's House), which has two rectangular towers. On the east side of the cathedral square the wall continues past the 15th-century almshouse, the **Pia Almoina**, running down Carrer de la Tapineria to Plaça Ramón Berenguer el Gran. The statue here of the 12th-century count, who added Provence to Catalonia by marriage, is by Josep Llimona (1864–1934).

Behind him is the facade of **Santa Agata**, growing from the Roman wall and including a Roman watchtower as the base for its bell-tower. This was the chapel of the complex that served as the count-kings' royal palace. To reach it, continue down Tapineria, turn right into Carrer Llibreteria, right again into Carrer Veguer and into the **Plaça del Rei**. This imposing square of solid door-ways and tawny towers, redolent of counts and courtiers, is the city's Gothic heart.

A tour of the complex should begin in the **Museu d'Història de la Ciutat** (City History Museum; Oct–May, 10am–2pm, 4–8pm, Sun 10am–2pm; Jun–Sep, 10am–8pm; closed Mon; entrance fee includes admission to the Royal Palace and Chapel). The exhibition rooms in the 17th-century Clariana-Padellàs merchant's house chart the development of the city. When this building was brought here, stone by stone, in 1930, Roman remains were excavated. Foundations of streets and houses, public baths, an oil factory and a burial ground in the basement of the museum extend beneath the square and beyond to the foundations of the cathedral.

The Royal Palace

On the opposite side of the square a fan-shaped flight of steps leads to the entrance of the **Palau Reial Major**. The building is mostly taken up by the **Saló del Tinell**, the Royal Palace's great hall on the left of the entrance. There has been a royal palace here since Visigothic times; the hall dates from the 11th century and its interior stone arches from the 14th century. This later, Gothic, work was carried out for Pere

Right: the tawny towers of the Plaça del Rei

III (the Ceremonious) by Guillem Carbonell, who was also responsible for much of the palace's facade. Columbus is said to have been received in the Tinell by Ferdinand and Isabella and this is where the Inquisition held its courts. Today it is a venue for concerts and exhibitions. To the right of the steps, built into the Roman wall is the Royal Chapel of **Santa Agata**, built for Jaume II (the Just) in 1312. His coat of arms is behind the fine retable of the Epiphany painted by Jaume Huguet in 1446.

A narrow flight of steps on the right of the nave leads up past the Saló del Tinell into the five-storey **Watchtower of Marti I**, the Humanist (1396–1410), who was the last of the 500-year dynasty of Catalan counts.

From here there is a great view across the old royal town.

The building on the left-hand side of the square is called the **Palau del Lloctinent**. The Lloctinent, or lord lieutenant, was the viceroy of Carlos V. The post was created in the late 18th century but the palace was built between 1549 and 1557 by Antoni Carbonell, and though it has such classic Catalan Gothic touches as the plain fan-stone portal, it is a Renaissance building. Its entrance is via the parallel Carrer dels Comtes where there is a splendid courtyard. Its rooms contain the Archives of the Crown of Aragon, which include monastic documents going back to the 9th century.

Above: historical costumes on display in the Museu Frederic Marès

Religious Artefacts

One further place in this royal complex needs to be visited, and that is the **Museu Frederic Marès** (Tue–Thur 10am–5pm, Wed, Fri–Sat 10am–6pm, Sun 10am–3pm, closed Mon; entrance fee). It lies directly behind the Tinell in what were the palace gardens; its entrance is a few metres further up the Carrer dels Comtes. This building started life in the 13th century as the bishop's palace, then became home to the counts of Barcelona and the count-kings of Barcelona-Aragon.

It now houses an extraordinary collection of mainly religious artefacts brought together by Marès, a wealthy local sculptor who had an apartment in the building and lived there until his death, at the age of 97, in 1991. There is a large Romanesque collection, particularly crucifixes, as well as entire portals. On the upper floors is a delightful hotchpotch of memorabilia from all ages of toys, pipes, locks, lacework, clocks, cameras and even pin-up postcards. The summer café in the courtyard is enchanting.

5. THE JEWISH QUARTER *(see pull-out map,)*

The narrow streets between La Rambla and the Cathedral, north of Carrer Ferran, still bear some traces of the city's medieval Jewish population, expelled 600 years ago.

As in many parts of the old city, the pleasure here is simply in walking the streets, peering into patios, window shopping, menu reading and wondering at the history heaped up behind walls of solid stone. Enter the Carrer Boqueria from La Rambla (Metro Line 3 to Liceu) and continue up the **Carrer del Call**, a lane of jewellers' shops. A Jewish quarter is a *call* in Catalan (the word comes from the Hebrew *qahqal*, meaning 'meeting'), and this is where a substantial population of the Jews lived from the 12th century. They were cultured teachers and prosperous merchants and they built the first university in Catalonia. In the 14th century, a build-up of anti-semitism led to the walling off of the *call* into a ghetto, with the only entrance at the end of Carrer del Call in Plaça Sant Jaume. In 1391, following widescale rioting in the wake of accusations that the Jews had brought the Black Death to Spain, the *call* was virtually destroyed, many of its residents murdered, and the rest given the choice of conversion or expulsion. This was a century before their religion was banned altogether.

From Carrer del Call turn up Sant Domènec del Call where some houses date back to the 12th century. The **main synagogue** was on the site of No 7, and a secondary synagogue was

Right: a street in the Jewish Quarter

built at the end of the street in 1379. Both sites are now private houses. Leading off are two lanes, Carrer Fruita and Carrer Marlet. In both streets the stonework is extraordinary: dressed and undressed; Roman slabs and lumpy cobbles. Windows and doorways are Romanesque and Gothic; some are bricked up. In the wall of No 1 Carrer Marlet, at the lower end, is a **Hebrew memorial stone** dated 1314 which reads simply: 'Holy foundation of Rabbi Samuel Hassardi for whom life never ends. Year 62'.

At the top of Carrer Sant Domènec del Call are Carrer Sant Sever and Baixada Santa Eulàlia, a continuous, sloping alley where furniture restorers work in sunless, cavernous basements. From Carrer Sant Sever there is access into the shady Plaça Sant Felip Neri where the **Museu del Calçat** (Museum of the History of Footwear) (11am–2pm, closed Mon; entrance fee) displays the largest shoe in the world, which was made to fit the statue of Christopher Columbus which stands on a tall plinth at the bottom of La Rambla. The collection also includes a gold stiletto-heeled shoe worn by the opera singer, Victoria de los Angeles.

Characterful Quarter

Turn back down Sant Domènec del Call and cross the Plaça Manuel Ribé to Carrer Arc Sant Ramón del Call, right into Carrer del Call and right again at the Obach shoe shop into **Carrer Banys Nous**, the 'Street of the New Baths'. Ramón Berenguer IV had public baths built here in 1160 and Jewish baths existed here until the early 19th century. This is one of the most characteristic streets of the old quarter, and among its commercial premises are a quaint dairy and one of the last of Barcelona's great *bodegas*, the **Portalón**.

At the top of this street turn left into Carrer de la Palla, which leads into **Plaça Sant Josep Oriol**. This delightful square has a weekend art market, and the adjoining **Plaça del Pi** has a local food produce market from Friday to Sunday on the first and third weeks of the month. Beside them rise the 14th-century **Santa María del Pi**, distinguished by its stained-glass windows.

Before settling for a drink in the square, a final detour should be made up Carrer Petritxol in the northwest corner of Plaça del Pi. This is an attractive street of art galleries. Sala Parés at No 5 dates from 1845, and was the first gallery to exhibit Picasso's work.

Above: an ornate facade in the Plaça del Pi
Right: the auditorium of the Palau de la Música Catalana

6. SECRETS OF THE OLD TOWN *(see map, p40)*

A less-trodden route through the Old Town, taking in historical highlights from Roman days to Modernisme, strolling through today's busy streets and ending in the latest and most indulgent of Barcelona's 80 museums, the Museu de la Xocolata.

Begin in Plaça Catalunya, at its best in the early morning light, and follow the short road between the two bastions of new colonisation in Barcelona, the Hard Rock Café and M & S, into the hidden square of Plaça Ramón Amadeu. At its far end the two-tiered Gothic cloisters of the medieval church of **Santa Anna** (Mon–Sat 9am–1pm, 6.30–8pm) are a haven from the surrounding commercial din. From the bustling street of Santa Anna go down Bertrellans, opposite the wonderful glove and fan shop *Guantería Alonso*, into **Plaça de la Vila de Madrid**. With luck the dazzling jacaranda will be in flower in this quiet square which has an overlooked treasure in its far corner: a Roman necropolis only discovered in the 1950s. Today, this ancient spot is neglected, a dormitory for the homeless and a playground for cats.

Follow Passatge Duc de la Victòria, one of the few cobbled streets left after 1990s urbanisation, to the Pèrgamon gallery (always worth a visit), go back up to Canuda and into Portal de l'Angel. A busy shopping area, ideal if you're hunting for shoes or moderately priced fashion, but best avoided on Saturday. Cut diagonally across it into Montsió. You'll know you've reached a tourist trap by the huddle of photographers around a Modernista building on the corner. Designed in 1897 by Puig i Cadafalch, **Casa Martí** became the famous café **Els Quatre Gats** (4 Cats), regularly frequented by Barcelona's artistic circle at the turn of the century, and where the 19-year-old Picasso had his first exhibition in 1900. You can try and catch the fervent atmosphere of the time by having the reasonably priced *menú* at lunchtime, but perhaps it is better to have a quick drink, absorb the decorative details and wander around the corner to a more genuine bar where the

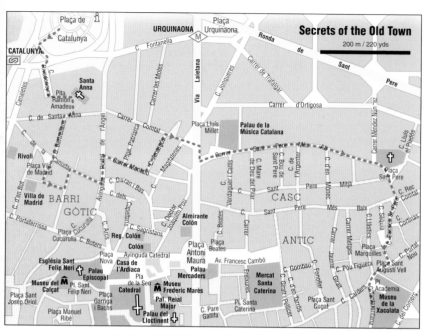

Secrets of the Old Town
200 m / 220 yds

locals eat, like Mercé de Vins in nearby **Amargós**. This narrow, pretty street takes a pride in itself, ceramic plaques sing its praises ('the first street in Barcelona to have paraffin lights') and the shops are unusual and attractive.

Silk, Music and Chocolate

Turn right at the end into Comtal and cross over busy, dusty Via Laietana into Sant Pere Més Alt, noticing at No 1 the fine example of *esgrafiat* (decorative relief work on the facade). This is Casal de Gremi de Velers (the Silk Industry Guild), marking the beginning of a *barri* still dedicated to the textile industry. A visit to the **Palau de la Música Catalana** is essential, either on a guided tour (daily 10.30am–3pm, later in summer) or by attending a concert. This extravaganza of Modernista architecture, built in 1908 by Domènech i Montaner, is still immensely popular as a concert hall despite the smart, recently opened Auditori (*see Itinerary 12, page 50*). After a lifetime crammed into the side of a church (it was built on the site of the former cloister) this bold, colourful building of tiles and mosaics, stained glass and statuary is emerging in all its splendour. The church has been demolished and new plans by Oscar Tusquets for a second stage underground and a patio for open-air concerts, allow maximum light into the original building.

The network of streets beyond, between Sant Pere Més Alt (Upper) and Sant Pere Més Baix (Lower), full of tiny drapers shops, is worth exploring. From **Plaça Sant Pere**, with an ancient church and Modernista fountain, take Basses Sant Pere to Plaça Sant Agustí Vell then Tantarantana to the final treat, the new **Museu de la Xocolata** (Comerç 36; Mon–Sat 10am–8pm, Sun till 3pm) in the old convent of Sant Agustí. In its *xocolateria* you can taste an authentic cup of hot chocolate.

city itineraries

7. EL RAVAL *(see map, p42)*

El Raval is the part of the old town on the opposite side of La Rambla to the Barri Gòtic, bounded by the Ronda de Sant Pau and the Avinguda Paral.lel. This tour takes in the city's oldest church and hospital as well as the ultra-modern Museu d'Art Contemporani de Barcelona (MACBA).

Neglected for years and ill-famed for drugs, delinquency and prostitution, this district, which includes the notorious Barri Xinès (or Barrio Chino), is undergoing a metamorphosis, aided by municipal funding. Trendy bars, shops and art galleries now mingle with what remains of 'local colour'. Until the 14th century this area lay outside the city and it has one of Europe's oldest hospitals and the city's oldest church. **Sant Pau del Camp** is at the western end of the Carrer de Sant Pau (Metro Line 3 to Paral.lel), one of the most characteristic streets of the impoverished Barri Xinès.

The present church has grown out of former Roman and Visigothic churches and was rededicated after the Moorish incursions of 1117. The lintel and marble capitals on the west portal are from the 7th century and the later Lombard bands (friezes of blind arches, which distinguish Catalan Romanesque) run along just below the roof. The **monastery** is approached through a door to the right of the church, which leads to a small, attractive cloister with cinquefoil and trefoil arches.

The chapter house and south transept lead off to the east side where a second-hand gravestone, used first for a Roman, bears an inscription to Guifre (Wilfred) II Borrell who in 897 became the second ruler of the Barcelona dynasty. He is the probable benefactor of the monastery. The church has a simple barrel vault. A marker shows the height of about 2m (6ft) that was reached by a flood in the city at 11.45pm on 21 August 1981.

Opposite the gate outside the church is the Carrer de les Carretes, a long straight lane overshadowed by balconies dripping washing and plants, which is one of the most typical streets in El Raval. There is no shortage of cafés and small bars if you feel like taking a break.

To Market

At the top of the street turn left and then right into Ronda de Sant Pau where you will immediately see the **Mercat de Sant Antoni** in one of the city's large, attractive iron halls (1882). During the week this serves as a food market, with clothes and haberdashers' stalls behind the encircling green blinds, and on Sunday morning there are book stalls to browse through (10am–2pm).

Right: the magnificent Romanesque doorway of Sant Pau del Camp

Take Carrers Sant Antoni Abat and Hospital back into El Raval from the market. This is a fascinating street of herbalists, pharmacists and second-hand clothes and junk shops. The 16th-century facade of the **Antic Hospital de la Santa Creu** soon looms up on the left and, just beyond it, La Capella, its small 15th-century church, which is now an exhibition space.

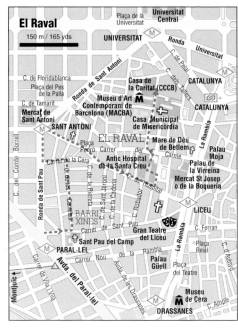

Through the main archway lie the former hospital grounds where people come to sit quietly, much as the convalescing patients must have done for 500 years. The convalescent house was set up here in the 15th century and it remained the city's principle hospital until Santa Creu i de Sant Pau was built in 1910 near Gaudí's Sagrada Família.

The hospital buildings are now devoted to the Massana Art School, Institute of Catalan Studies and the Library of Catalonia. Walk through to the second square and on the left you will see an entrance into the **Convalescence House Gardens**, richly decorated with coloured tiles by Llorens Passolles in 1681.

Modern Art

Leave the hospital by the nearby north gate, turning left down Carrer del Carme. Cross the road and turn up Carrer dels Angels through the Plaça Angels to the ice-white **Museu d'Art Contemporani de Barcelona** (MACBA) (noon–8pm; Sat 10am–8pm; Sun 10am–3pm; closed Tue; entrance fee) designed by American architect Richard Meier. It's a brilliant space on three floors showing post-war Catalan and Spanish art, and temporary exhibitions

Beside it, in the old Casa de Caritat (once a poorhouse and orphanage), is the **Centre de Cultura Contemporània** (CCCB; Tue, Thur, Fri 11am–2pm, 4–8pm; Wed, Sat 11am–8pm; Sun 11am–7pm; entrance fee), a series of exhibition spaces that has a stimulating programme of exhibitions, concerts, dance and films.

Left: one of El Raval's trendy second-hand shops
Right: the *Amérigo Vespucci* in the harbour

8. PORT VELL *(see map, p44)*

From the Drassanes Museu Marítim to Barceloneta, around the city's revitalised old port.

Port Vell, the old port of Barcelona, is a focal point of leisure pursuits centred on the Moll d'Espanya where the Maremàgnum shopping, restaurant and cinema complex, L'Aquàrium and Imax cinema have added glamour to the old yachting basin. Vessels from the city's two yacht clubs have to wait for the swing bridge to open on the pedestrian Rambla de Mar, to let them out into the sea. As with any port there is always activity, among the gin palaces and visiting tall ships in the Marina Esportiva, the cruise liners on the Moll de Barcelona, the trawlers in Barceloneta and the pleasure boats that conduct trips round the port.

The Old Shipyards

The nearest Metro stop is Drassanes at the bottom of the Rambla (Line 3). This is the name of the city's former shipyards, which have been refurbished as a museum, the **Museu Marítim** (10am–7pm, Tue–Fri in summer 10am–10pm; entrance fee), a good place to begin a tour of maritime Barcelona. Situated beyond the end of La Rambla, on the right, the revitalised shipyards are enclosed by the city's 15th-century outer wall, which stretches round into Avinguda del Paral.lel where the Portal de Santa Madrona tower and gateway also remain.

The Drassanes is the place that launched a thousand ships, a soaring cathedral of *naves*. The sheds, put up in 1378 and greatly enlarged in the 17th century, were the first arsenal in Spain, preceded in the Mediterranean only by Venice. At their height they were turning out 30 war galleys at a time, which they were hastily doing as the Christian west prepared for a final showdown with the Muslim Ottomans in 1571 at Lepanto off the Greek coast. A full-scale replica of Don John's victorious flagship, the *Reial*, is the centrepiece of the museum. This great golden galley, with banks of oars to drive it head-on into its foe, bore the *Lepanto Christ*, a crucifix now in Barcelona cathedral. The museum, which spreads throughout the large, impressive halls charts Catalonia's sea-faring history through its interactive exhibition 'The Great Sea Adventure' as well as showing a collection of fishing

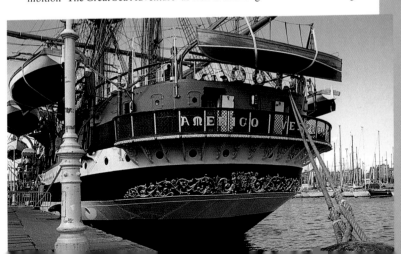

boats, model naval ships, ceramics and documents mostly from Catalonia, but some from other parts of the world.

The nearby **Monument a Colom**, the Columbus Monument, is a traffic island, and the reward for patiently waiting to cross to it is a ride up the internal lift to a viewing platform at the top of this 60-m (200-ft) column, open most daylight hours. It was designed by Gaietà Buïgas, with a crowning sculpture of the Genoan navigator by Rafael Arché, for the Universal Exhibition of 1888. It stands in the Plaça Portal de la Pau (Gate of Peace Square) through which Christopher Columbus, his wife, three sons, seven Carib Indians and fellow explorers entered the city on his return from the West Indies in April 1493.

In front of the statue is the waterfront Moll de les Drassanes where the *golondrina* (swallow) pleasure boats offer trips to the entrance of the harbour or to the Olympic port. To the left is the **Junta d'Obres del Port**, the Port Authority building constructed in 1907 as a reception point for passengers.

Go over the wooden Rambla de Mar to the Moll d'Espanya, the main jetty of Port Vell. The cinema and shopping complex of **Maremàgnum**, with plenty of places for refreshment, leads to **L'Aquarium** (summer, daily 9.30am–10pm; winter, daily 10am–9pm; entrance fee). This underwater world shows what snorkel divers are likely to see in the surrounding seas, and an imaginative tunnel leads visitors among sharks and rays.

The promenade beyond the Junta d'Obres on the shore is the old timber wharf, the **Moll de la Fusta**, redesigned by Manuel de Solà-Morales – a place to stroll by day and dance by night in its various bars.

On the other side of the Moll d'Espanya is the Marina Esportiva, in former times a dock area with bustling warehouses. The only one left is Elies

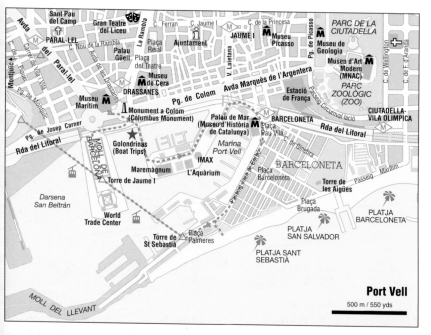

Port Vell

500 m / 550 yds

Rogent's 1878 Magatzem General, now the **Palau del Mar**. There are restaurants where you can sit outside, and part of the building is the excellent **Museu d'Historia de Catalunya** (Tue–Thur 10am–7pm; Fri–Sat 10am–8pm; Sun 10am–2.30pm; entrance fee), with lots of child-friendly interactive exhibits.

Cable Car Ride

To complete the round trip of Port Vell, you could stroll down to the Torre de Sant Sebastià cable car. A lift ascends the iron hulk of a tower to a platform where the enclosed buckets of the **Aeri del Port** fly over the harbour towards the World Trade Center and the cruise ship terminal on the Moll de Barcelona. You could get off here and head back to the Columbus Monument; alternatively, wander through Barceloneta's streets to reach the city's closest beaches *(see Itinerary 13, page 52)*.

9. CIUTADELLA PARK *(see pull-out map)*

Within this peaceful park's boundaries are several museums and cultural centres, the Catalan parliament and the zoo.

The 34-ha (75-acre) **Parc de la Ciutadella** is the largest breathing space near the old city, and its zoological and geological museums and zoo make it a good place for children. Its many varieties of trees are well labelled, and the palms attract squawking parrots escaped from their cages on La Rambla. The park takes its name from a star-shaped citadel built by Felipe V after besieging the city in 1714. Most of this fortress was later torn down and the park was laid out in 1873 by Josep Fontseré. The Ciutadella-Vila Olímpica Metro (Line 4) is on its south side in the Olympic Village, but only has access to the park via the zoo.

A better option is **Arc de Triomf** (Line 1) on the north side, at the end of Passeig de Lluís Companys where the city's law courts are. The station is named after an arch that echoes the one in Paris. It was designed by Josep Vilaseca i Casanovas as the entrance to the Universal Exhibition of 1888. Most of the exhibition buildings were hastily erected and not meant to last, with the notable exception of Lluís Domènech i Montaner's **Café-Restaurant**.

This castle-like building, modelled on the Llotja (Stock Exchange) in Valencia, was an arts and crafts centre for a while and set the young architects of Barcelona on the path towards Modernisme.

Today a visitor may be forgiven for thinking this crenellated red-brick fort, more often known as the **Castell del Tres Dragons** (Castle of the Three Dragons), is

Left: the Columbus Monument
Right: a detail on the Arc de Triomf

the citadel after which the park is named. Impossible to miss, it is on the edge of the park beside the Passeig de Picasso. A parliament assembled here in 1917. In 1934, it became the **Museu de Zoologia**, the Zoological Museum (10am–2pm; closed Mon; entrance fee), which has a Victorian collection of stuffed animals. To the south is the **Museu de Geologia** or Geology Museum (10am–2pm; closed Mon; entrance fee), bright with crystals, minerals and fossils, in a neoclassical building. On either side of the museum lie the greenhouses of the **Hivernacle**, an idyllic setting for summer concerts, and Fontseré's **Umbracle**, a palm house. Just outside in Passeig de Picasso is the glass cube entitled *Homenatje a Picasso,* by Antoni Tàpies.

Five minutes' walk away is the centre of the park and the **Plaça d'Armes** where *Sorrow*, by Josep Llimona, crouches in the central pond. The build-

ings each side of it are all that remain of the citadel built by the victorious Bourbon king, Felipe V. They were used as a prison, captured by Napoleon, demolished, rebuilt, handed back to the town and bombed in the civil war. On the west side is a small chapel and beside it is the former local governor's palace of 1748, now a school.

Government and Art

On the opposite, eastern, side of the square is the former arsenal, which was made a royal palace when the park became a leisure ground in the late 19th century. The **Catalan parliament** occupies most of it and, as one guide has it, in 'the extreme left wing' is the **Museu d'Art Modern** (10am–7pm; Sun 10am–2.30pm; closed Mon; entrance fee). The individual galleries for Barcelona's most illustrious painters elsewhere in the city have deprived this collection of works by Miró, Picasso, Dalí and Tàpies, but there are some interesting pieces to be seen. These include the works of Santiago Rusiñol (1861–1931) and Ramón Casas (1866–1932), prime movers in early 20th-century Catalan art and Catalonia's other important 19th-century painters, Fortuny, Mir and Nonell. There are a number of figurative sculptures by Josep Llimona and Miquel Blay and several rooms devoted to Modernist furniture and interior design.

Barcelona **Zoo** (daily 9.30am–7.30pm; entrance fee) is just to the south. There are elephants, hippos, big cats and performing dolphins. The most famous inmate is the ageing Snowflake (Floc de Neu), the only albino gorilla in captivity. In front of the zoo there is a fountain with a sculpture of a young woman holding an umbrella which keeps the water from her elegant clothes. Called the *Dama del Paraigues*, by Roig i Soler it is a kind of mascot of the city.

Above: there are regular dolphin shows at the Barcelona Zoo

10. ¡BARÇA! *(see map, p48)*

A visit to Barcelona's football stadium and museum.

After the Picasso Museum, the Barcelona football club museum is the most visited in the city. Fans from all over the world come to see Europe's largest stadium, to wonder at the trophies, watch the playbacks, gloat over past glories and stand in the directors' box. The stadium, called **Camp Nou** (New Field), has been extended since it was built in 1957 and can now hold some 100,000. It is the largest constituent part of a sports complex just below the university campus and the smart end of Avinguda Diagonal. Basketball, hockey, handball, junior football and ice hockey are also catered for in its neighbouring buildings, the **Mini Estadi**, the **Palau Blaugrana** (*blau* translates as blue, *grana* as burgundy: the club colours) and the **Pista de Gel** ice rink.

Ticket First

Take the Metro (Line 3) and get off at Las Corts, or take Line 5 to Collblanc. Turn immediately up Francesc Layret and right into Travessera de les Corts, then second left beside the perimeter fence up Carrer d'Arístides Maillol. The main ticket office is on this corner and tickets are on sale week days 9am–1pm, 4–8pm. Same-day tickets can be bought in ticket offices on Avinguda Les Corts or Avinguda Joan XXIII. Match times vary between 5 and 9pm (usually on Sunday) according to the time of year. *Entrada general* are the cheapest tickets for the top tier of the stadium. *Lateral* are good, middle-priced seats and *Tribuna* are the covered, more expensive seats.

Continue up Arístides Maillol and turn right into the souvenir shop to buy tickets for the **museum** (Mon–Sat 10am–6.30pm; Sun 10am–2pm; entrance fee). Your ticket gives access to the marble directors' box where it is easy to believe that this is the world's richest football club with the highest membership in the world: about 100,000 have permanent seats in the ground. The museum includes a trophy room, video viewing room, posters, paintings and other memorabilia. Return the way you came; if you want to visit the Pedralbes Palace and Monastery just north of here, *see Itinerary 11, page 48*.

Above: a floodlit match at Camp Nou

11. PEDRALBES PALACE AND MONASTERY *(see map below)*

A route that also includes the Museu de Ceràmica, the Thyssen-Bornemisza art collection and the Güell estate.

Pedralbes is without doubt the finest surviving monastery in the city. Set in what has become one of the wealthiest districts, it nevertheless has a pleasant, away-from-it-all feeling. Within walking distance of the monastery along roads lined with high-priced apartments is **Palau Reial de Pedralbes**. This can provide a starting point for the tour. The Palau Reial Metro (Line 3) emerges outside the entrance to the palace grounds, which are small formal Italianate gardens with sculptures and ponds. The Renaissance-style palace was built by the city council in 1925 to attract visits from King Alfonso XIII, who went into exile six years later. The main part of the palace is not open to the public, and the royal family use it occasionally for banquets and receptions. The **Museu de Ceràmica** and the **Museu de les Arts Decoratives** (10am–6pm; Sun 10am–3pm; closed Mon; entrance fee includes both museums) are currently housed here.

There are some beautiful plates, pots and tiles, some from other parts of Spain, some Islamic, dating back to the 9th century. Up-

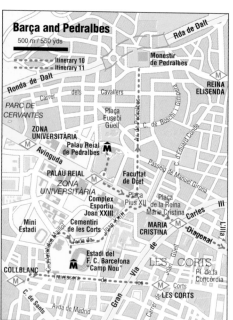

Barça and Pedralbes

500 m / 550 yds

- - - - Itinerary 10
········· Itinerary 11

Rda de Dalt
Ronda de Dalt
Monestir de Pedralbes
REINA ELISENDA
PARC DE CERVANTES
Carrer dels Cavallers
Plaça Eusebi Güell
ZONA UNIVERSITÀRIA
Avinguda
Palau Reial de Pedralbes
PALAU REIAL
ZONA UNIVERSITÀRIA
Facultat de Dret
Complex Esportiu Joan XXIII
Plaça Pius XII
Plaça de la Reina Maria Cristina
MARIA CRISTINA
Carles
Diagonal
C. de Bosch
C. d'Eduard Conde
Passeig de Manuel Girona
Mini Estadi
Cementiri de les Corts
Avda de
Estadi del F. C. Barcelona "Camp Nou"
LES CORTS
Pl. de la Concòrdia
COLLBLANC
Travessera
de
Corts
LES CORTS
Gran
Via
Joan Güell
C. de Sants
Ayda de Madrid

Above: the serene and lovely Pedralbes Monastery

stairs the contemporary rooms have a few works by Picasso, Artigas and Miró. In the Decorative Arts museum are collections of pocket watches and Spanish glass. Its industrial design collection is the first in Spain. Before it was transformed into a palace, this building was a pavilion on the holiday estate of the wealthy Güell family. The rest of the family's estate, for which Gaudí designed a lodge, stable and riding school, is situated behind the palace. Turn left outside the main gate, left up Avinguda de Pedralbes beside the Law Faculty (Barcelona's finest example of the International Style), and left again around the back of the Passeig de Til.lers. Immediately visible is the entrance gate to the **Güell estate**, a tortuous iron work by Gaudí featuring a dragon.

Continue up Avinguda de Pedralbes to the **monastery**, unmissable at the top. The enclave of gold–stoned buildings is penetrated through an arch up a cobbled street. The old monastery is on the left, approached through the museum entrance, which is also the entrance to the Thyssen-Bornemisza Collection *(see below)*. The three-storey cloister is Catalan-Gothic at its most elegant. In the gardens are fruit trees, and former nuns' cells lead off around the sides. The most beautifully decorated cell belonged to the queen's niece. It was painted by Ferrer Bassa in 1346. The monastery was built for Queen Elisenda de Montcada, wife of Jaume II the Just, when she came to live here in religious isolation after his death in 1327.

In those days the sick were tended in the **infirmary**, in four rooms which are now simply furnished as if they were still occupied. Interesting, too, is the **refectory**, with a long table laid out as if for the Last Supper. Beside it are the kitchens, blue-tiled and stone-sinked. The whole place is suffused with atmosphere and it is easy to imagine daily monastic life.

Velázquez and El Greco

The former dormitory and the palace's main hall now houses the **Collección Thyssen Bornemisza** (10am–2pm; closed Mon; entrance fee). It includes religious paintings by Velázquez, El Greco, Zubarán, Rubens, Tintoretto and other great masters.

When you leave the museum, continue up the side of the building to reach the entrance to the **church**. This simple Gothic building contains Queen Elisenda's marble tomb. Part of the nave at the back of the church, behind a grille, is used by the 19 nuns who still live in Pedralbes – their number has declined in recent years.

To return to the centre of Barcelona, turn left immediately outside the entrance arch and follow the road down to the Reina Elisenda FGC station. Or take the No 22 bus from Plaça de Pedralbes (turn left outside the monastery) to Avinguda del Tibidabo for a trip to the hilltop amusement park *(see Itinerary 14, page 53)*.

Right: a painted tile in the Pedralbes cloister

12. GLORIES TO POBLE NOU *(see map, p51)*

An interesting walk off the beaten track, from the new cultural complex in Glòries to Poble Nou, an industrial area in transition, ending at the beaches beyond the Olympic Village.

Take the Plaça de les Glòries Catalanes exit from Metro Glòries and have a quick look at this park created in the no-man's land of an elaborate traffic junction. A rather abandoned example of the new urban planning from the 1980s and 1990s, it is like an arena, with one exit to Els Encants flea market (Mon, Wed, Fri, Sat 8am–7pm) and another to the unprepossessing Glòries shopping centre. Return to the one leading to the Jardins del Bosquet dels Encants, a microcosmic Mediterranean wood, pleasant on a hot day despite rather more litter than is usually found in a Mediterranean wood.

Wander through to have a closer look at the **Teatre Nacional de Catalunya** (TNC), the National Theatre, opened in 1998, a larger than life neoclassical monument, designed by Ricardo Bofill. Performances are generally in Catalan, but the dance season is more accessible to visitors. Just beyond it is Rafael Moneo's **L'Auditori** opened in 1999, home of the Barcelona Orchestra (OBC) with a 2,500-seat symphonic hall and a smaller space for chamber music.

Industrial Relics

From this cultural complex you could head straight down the streets Pamplona or Zamora to the Olympic Village and its beaches, but for a fascinating insight into Barcelona's industrial past and present and a look at a popular neighbourhood, zig-zag down through **Poble Nou**. As the street layout has a similar grid system to the Eixample you can vary the route without fear of getting lost and be rewarded by finding gems – a timeless ironmonger's, a friendly corner bar with a cheap *menú,* a crumbling old factory with a beautiful chimney (not many left) – just keep heading down and across.

Or try this: from Avinguda Meridiana follow Bolivia for two blocks then turn right into Ávila past the new headquarters of the *mossos d'Esquadra* (Catalonia's autonomous police force) in an enormous renovated 1930s

textile factory (notice the original windows at the rear). Turn left into Tànger and on the corner of Ciutat de Granada there is a fine example of an early 20th century wool factory, salvaged and born again with a 21st-century function as the Catalan Institute of Technology. Go down a few blocks past Restaurante Mi Casa with its tables under the plane trees. The discreet, pretty building on the corner of Pere IV is the design and cutting centre of Josep Font, one of Catalonia's leading dress designers. This mixture of an industrial past (particularly in textiles: Poble Nou used to be known as the Catalan Manchester), a residue of light industry, new businesses opening, long-term residents and new apartment blocks, is fascinating. Some ruined factories are waiting to be devoured by property developers; others are being carefully preserved and trendily renovated to accommodate design studios or residential lofts.

Turn left into Pallars, Pujades or Llull, and three blocks on is the gentle bustle of pretty **Rambla de Poble Nou**, with some *Modernista* buildings and the atmosphere of a provincial town, with elderly folk taking the air with their grandchildren, and gossiping with their neighbours.

Follow the Rambla down towards the sea, pausing for a *orxata* or ice cream at Tio Che on the corner of Ramón Turró, or an excellent *tapa* at Bar Lovento (No 21). Take a left turn into Fernando Poo to the **Plaça Prim** with its pleasing, albeit relatively expensive, Els Pescadors restaurant. You can get to the Mar Bella beach through the Parc Poblenou. Take a final look at the few remaining chimneys, which are rapidly being consumed by major construction: this is Diagonal Mar, a new residential area. On the seafront another venture is taking shape: the Forum 2004, a Universal Forum of Cultures, is Barcelona's next great challenge.

Left: the sparkling new National Theatre
Above: enjoying one of the city's beaches

13. THE BEACHES *(see pull-out map)*

Along the beaches from Barceloneta to the Port Olímpic.

The beaches that extend north from Barceloneta comprise one of the major legacies of the 1992 Olympic Games. Before the regeneration programme began, this was an industrial area to be avoided, and few people ventured here for a dip. The whole area was planned as a smart new residential quarter and designed by various star architects. Its 2,000 apartments in six-storey blocks covering 63ha (160 acres) were first used as the Vila Olímpic for athletes' accommodation. The new ring-road (Ronda Literal) runs through it and the main railway line to France, leaving from the refurbished Estació de França, has been hidden underground. Now there are over 5km (3 miles) of sandy beaches, a smart new promenade and a leisure port with a bigger concentration of restaurants than just about anywhere else in Europe.

Old and New

Start at **Barceloneta**, take your swimming togs, and don't forget some cash for a proper lunch. The fishing harbour is marked by a clock tower that once served as a lighthouse and nearby is the fish market (weekdays 6am and 5pm). Barceloneta was created in 1753 to house the citizens who had been usurped by the building of the Ciutadella fortress. The architect of the low-rise houses built in a grid system that allowed volleys from the castle to be directed straight down their streets, was a military engineer, Juan Martín de Cermeño, who also designed **Sant Miquel del Port**, the local church.

The twin towers of the Arts Hotel and the MAPFRE commercial building are the highpoints of what was the Olympic Village, the housing estate that replaced the industrial wasteland. Heading along the beach or promenade towards them, you will pass on your left, just before reaching the hospital, the singular remains of this once dusty industrial spot: a gasometer skele-

Above: the beaches at Barceloneta have been cleaned up and become fashionable

ton and an elaborate *Modernista* **Water Tower** designed by Josep Domènech Estapá (1905).

In front of the twin towers is a giant, bronze-glinting metal fish, *Pez y Esfera* by Frank Gehry, which rises above Planet Hollywood at the edge of the **Port Olímpic**. Each of the quays is named after one of the local winds: Mestral, Gregal, Xaloc. Along two of them, on two levels, there are nothing but restaurants. Spilling over the quaysides are fish restaurants, ham restaurants and *tapes* bars – every kind of taste is catered for.

Beyond the port are more restaurants on the sea front, calling themselves *chirringuitos*, or shacks, a reference to the characterful beach restaurants of Barceloneta that were sacrificed during the making of the bright new seafront.

14. TIBIDABO FUNFAIR *(see map, p54)*

Via the Science Museum up to the city's lofty amusement park.

According to the Bible, the devil took Christ up into 'an exceeding high mountain and sheweth him all the kingdoms of the world, and the glory of them; And saith unto him, All these things *I will give thee* [*tibi dabo*] if thou wilt fall down and worship me.'

Tibidabo is the 517-m (1,700-ft) summit of the Collserola hills that hang behind the city. From here the view down over the world's glories, across Barcelona to the sea and the Balearic islands, north to the Pyrenees and west to Montserrat, is fantastic on about one day a year. But even with the traffic haze above the city there is a fine view of the skyline pricked by the cathedral, the Sagrada Família and the skyscrapers of the Olympic village. An afternoon or evening out here can be a family occasion, taking in Tibidabo's amusement park and having hands-on fun at the Science Museum.

Getting up the hill is part of the pleasure. Take the FGC train to Avinguda Tibidabo station, walk up the Avinguda del Tibidabo taking the first left and following the Carrer Teodor Roviralta round to the right and up to the **Museu de la Ciència**, the Science Museum (10am–8pm; closed Mon; entrance fee). Some of the 19th-century mansions that line the streets from here have been turned into restaurants.

The museum is full of things to do. There are energy and force machines and computers test your reflexes, equilibrium, colour awareness and ability to leap. There are microscopes and satellite pictures and a submarine to walk around. The higher than normal entrance fee probably reflects the wear and tear that these machines suffer from parties of school children.

Right: the ornate Sagrat Cor church on top of Tibidabo

Return to the bottom of the street to the bus stop beside the **Hospital Sant Gervasi**, the former Rotonda Hotel with a *Modernista* minaret. From here a bus, or sometimes the more interesting Tramvia Blau (Blue Tram) goes to the Funicular, where two old wooden tram cars grind up the steep hill every 30 minutes. Their destination is the **Parc d'Atraccions** (times vary through the year; usually noon–10pm; closes later at weekends) at the top of the hill, with a big wheel, helter skelter and white-knuckle rides including the Pasaje del Terror and the Avion Tibiair, a red aeroplane that swoops off the side of the hill into empty space. There is also a museum of mechanical toys. There is an entrance fee (except for under-5s) and rides must be paid for as well, although all-inclusive tickets are available.

City Views

It is not obligatory to visit the funfair on Tibidabo. There are restaurants on the hill, with fine views, and pleasant paths to walk. Above is the **Sagrat Cor**, the Sacred Heart church, a 20th-century confection from which it is possible – via the lift in the tower – to enjoy even better views of this dynamic city. For an even loftier view, take the lift up to the glassed-in observation platform on the tenth floor of the 288-m (945-ft) **Communications Tower** (11am–2.30pm, 3.30–8pm; all day at weekends). Designed by British architect Norman Foster, this is sometimes known locally as Torre Foster.

You can also use Tibidabo as local people do, as a retreat from the city. It crowns the Collserola massif, some 8,000ha (19,700 acres) of woodland, where you can walk, cycle, picnic, or explore typical Catalan country houses.

Above: an inviting, old-fashioned sign at the museum of mechanical toys
Right: all the fun of the fair

Excursions

1. SITGES *(see pull-out map)*

The first man in Spain to pursue swimming as a leisure activity was the fin-de-siècle artist Santiago Rusiñol. He took the plunge in Sitges, a pretty fishing village 40km (25 miles) south of Barcelona, and anyone in the city in summer today will feel a need to follow his example.

Although the best known of the capital's local resorts, easily reached in a day trip, **Sitges** remains a pretty and civilised place. A former wine town which had trade links with America, it prospered in the 19th century, when so-called Indianos, local people who had gone abroad to find their fortune, had come home wealthy to retire in mansions and build summer houses. Barcelona's new bourgeoisie found their way here, too. The Luminist School of Sitges preceded Rusiñol and the Modernists, but when this energetic artist and writer bought his home here in 1891, Sitges was dubbed by the Barcelona press as 'the Mecca of Modernism'. Later, the Spanish poet and playwright Federico García Lorca (1899–1936) came to stay, as did the French composer Erik Satie (1866–1925). Subsequent regular visitors included the English writer G.K. Chesterton (1874–1936), to whom the town has erected a statue. In the late 1950s and early 1960s Sitges responded to the coast's great tourist influx by providing a wide range of pubs and bars and a few hotels; local people rented out rooms in summer and a few entrepreneurs built modest apartment blocks, but no high-rises followed and, in the main, development has been contained.

Getting There

The resort is highly accessible from the capital. The A16 motorway (toll) has been blasted through the Garraf mountains to alleviate the congested *autovia* that winds along by the sea south from Barcelona. Trains, sometimes double-deckers, leave from the central Sants or Passeig de Gràcia stations every 30 minutes. Fast trains take 25 minutes; others, stopping at nearly every station, take almost twice as long. The tourist office is in the Passeig de Vilafranca outside the station. If possible avoid summer weekends, when the town is at its busiest.

Like most resorts on the coast, it has several beaches. Sant Sebastià is to the north; further south are the Platjes dels Morts, two nude beaches, one for heterosexuals, one for gays. The main beach, however, the **Platja d'Or**, is the great attraction, and the visitor should head straight down to it from the station. The clean sandy strand is 5km (3 miles) long, backed by a palm-lined promenade and overlooked from the north by the distinctive facade of the 17th-century church, Sant Bartomeu i Santa Tecla.

Left: stunning colours in the Museu Maricel
Right: tourist information in Sitges

The liveliest thoroughfare is the **Carrer Primer de Maig**, which runs back from the middle of the promenade. This street of bars is known as the **Carrer del Pecat** (Sin Street) and it is here that Sitges' main annual festivities reach their height. At Corpus Christi (in late June) carpets of flowers cover the street, but its most vibrant time is during pre-Lent carnival, when there is an elaborate show of costume and design. The Shrove Tuesday evening parade is the most outrageous, when transvestites take centre stage.

At the top of Primer de Maig turn right and then left up Carrer Sant Josep to find the **Museu Romàntic** (9.30am–2pm, 4–9pm, 4–6pm in winter; Sun 9.30am–2pm; closed Mon; entrance fee) on the corner of Carrer Sant Gaudenci. This house, built in 1793 by the cultured Llopis family, was given to the town complete with what must then have been a contemporary museum of family life. Period interiors such as this are unusual in the region.

Return down Sant Josep and turn left into Carrer Parellades and continue down to Carrer Major – or take any agreeable little street back down towards the church at the top end of the beach. A cannon here bears a plaque explaining that it saw off two English frigates that had their eyes on cargo ships anchored in the bay. Continue round the back of the church into Carrer Fonoller. The town now takes on a wealthy air: the magnificent white mansions seem to belong to an affluent city rather than a seaside resort.

Rusiñol's Home

On the left is the **Palau Maricel**, with a roof terrace of lovely blue tiles. On the right is Rusiñol's home, **Cau Ferrat**. Like many artists of his generation, he was funded by his family – his had grown rich in Barcelona's industrial revolution. He travelled frequently to Paris, forging important links for local artists. He bought this building, run-down at the time, to house his collection of ironwork and to use as a studio, and between 1892

Above: the distinctive facade of Sitges' main church lords it over the crowded beach

and 1899 he put on the *Festes Modernistes*, festivals of painting, sculpture, concerts, plays and dance. His widow left the **Museu Cau Ferrat** to the town (9.30am–2pm, 4–6pm, Sun 9.30am–2pm; closed Mon; entrance fee). The collection is a bright and cheerful one. It includes two El Grecos (which Rusiñol bought in Paris and which were carried through the town like venerated statues in a mock Holy Week procession), five small Picassos and an intriguing double portrait painted by both Rusiñol and Ramón Casas, Modernist painting's other great exponent.

A ticket to the Cau Ferrat museum also entitles the visitor to a guided tour of the neighbouring **Museu Maricel**. This former hospital was renovated by the critic and artist, Miquel Utrillo, a founder, along with Rusiñol and Casas, of Barcelona's Quatre Gats café *(see page 39)*. This museum is taken up with a collection of Gothic paintings, but the interior decoration is lovely.

North of this collection of imposing buildings is the beach of Sant Sebastià. Quieter than the main beach, it offers good restaurants, with pavement cafésa. But there are also plenty of restaurants and bars to visit along the main waterfront, around the Carrer Primer de Maig, and in pretty back streets.

2. CAVA COUNTRY *(see pull-out map)*

An excursion 40km (25 miles) south of Barcelona into the Penedès wine-producing region.

Catalonia's gift to the world's table is *Cava*, a sparkling wine produced in exactly the same way as Champagne, but forbidden the French appellation by the EU and the lawyers from Rheims. The ruling of the European courts is likely to turn out to be in the wine's favour, for the word *Cava* has been seeping into foreign languages as a word that means very good, inexpensive, earthy, non-acid sparkling wine. Around 90 percent of the country's output comes from the Penedès region, to the south of Barcelona, in vineyards around the towns of Vilafranca del Penedès and Sant Sadurní d'Anoia.

Some travel agencies and tour operators organise visits to the producers, though the most comprehensive information on visits to the over 300 wine and *Cava* producers in the area is the Vilafranca Tourist Office (Cort 14; www.ajvilafranca.es). However, it is also perfectly possible to visit both towns independently in a day out, and gain a flavour not just of the product but of the countryside. Leaving Barcelona, take the A7 motorway which passes both towns, or a RENFE train from Plaça Catalunya or Sants station. As with Catalan businesses, most of the wine houses are closed in August.

Begin the bacchanalian tour in **Sant Sadurní d'Anoia**. Near the station is the **Freixenet** house, one of the largest in the region (Mon–Fri tours at 9am, 10am, 11.30am, Mon–Thur also 3.30pm, 5.30pm). More impressive, however, is the out-

LA PLAÇA MÉS CASTELLERA

Right: wall tiles in Vilafranca celebrate the *castellers*

of-town **Codorníu** house (9am–5pm; weekends 9am–1.30pm; closed July 22 and August 21), signposted and about 20 minutes' walk from the station. This is the home of *Cava*. Josep Raventós, of the Cordoníu family dynasty, popped the first *Cava* cork here in 1872. His son Manuel took over the firm 13 years later after the vine phylloxera louse had devastated the region. He replanted and rebuilt the vineyards and buildings, adding the huge *Modernista* cellars designed by Puig i Cadafalch and now a national monument. The tour of the cellars starts here, and includes an explanation of the method involved, video shows and a train ride through part of the five storeys of cellars that cover a total of 26km (16 miles).

Sant Sadurní is a small country town without much activity. A plaque on the town hall commemorates a visit by King Juan Carlos and Queen Sofía in 1987, on the centenary of the first *Cava* production after the phylloxera blight had been eradicated. At the top of the main road, Carrer Jacint Verdaguer, is Mon del Cava, a large shop where anyone wanting to start up their own wine-making can buy presses, bottles and barrels.

Human Pyramids

For lunch it may be best to head on to **Vilafranca del Penedès** some 15 minutes away by train, a little longer by bus. There are some good restaurants by the station, or try the restaurant the locals go to, **La Llar de La Villa** in the Rambla de Sant Francesc, or sit at the marble-topped tables in the pretty **Coro** in the **Plaça de Constitució**: it is not hard to find your way around town. This last square has wall tiles celebrating the *castellers*, human pyramids that are a custom of the region. They gather here at the end of August and, physically supported by the crowds, compete for height, balance and skill.

'*Hi ha Cava a copes*' all the bars proclaim: 'There is *Cava* by the glass here'. But in fact Vilafranca is the centre for still wine production. The old

bodega of the great **Torres** family is at 22 Carrer de Commercio, near the station, though you can also visit their state-of-the-art winery out of town.

The **Museu del Vi**, Spain's best wine museum (summer, 9am–9pm, Sun 10am–2pm; winter, 10am–2pm and 4–7pm; closed Mon; entrance fee includes tasting) is situated among several Gothic buildings in the Plaça Jaume I, opposite the basilica of Santa María, in a former palace of the count-kings of Catalonia-Aragon. It has various implements from the industry's past, and a bar displays the region's wine. The building also houses a collection of ceramics, archaeology and art.

If you have your own transport, you can visit **Sitges**, 22km (14 miles) south on the coast *(see Excursion 1, page 57)*. There is also a bus service, but there is no rail link.

Left: a market in Sant Sadurní

3. DISCOVERING DALI *(see pull-out map)*

A trip to Dalí country, beginning in Figueres, about 1½ hours' drive from Barcelona, then on to Port Lligat some 30 km/18 miles away, returning via the castle of Púbol, near Girona. Figueres is accessible by train but you need private transport and an overnight stop if you want to visit all three sites.

The art treasures of Barcelona, ancient and modern, often engender an interest in Catalunya's most extravagant artist, the Surrealist Salvador Dalí. This excursion takes you to three museums dedicated to his life and work. The first is in the market town of **Figueres**, where the artist was born in 1904, the son of a public notary. Many of his major works are displayed in the **Teatre-Museu Dalí** (1 Jul–30 Sep, daily 9am–7.15pm, 1 Oct–30 Jun, 10.30am–5.15pm, closed Mon; entrance charge). Set in the Plaça Gala-Sal-

vador Dalí, to the north of the town's main rambla, the museum was constructed on the site of a municipal theatre that was burned down in 1939, at the end of the Civil War. Dalí died in the adjoining Torre Galatea in 1989 and he is buried in the crypt.

Among the extraordinary works here are the *Poetry of America*, or *Cosmic Athletes*, painted in 1943, a portrait of Gala as *Atomic Leda*, and the huge ceiling fresco dominating the *Wind Palace Room* on the first floor. In the garden, the *Rainy Taxi* sculpture is a crowd puller. This is one of the few art galleries that small children generally enjoy – its quirkiness appeals to their sense of the ridiculous.

It is advisable to avoid visiting the museum on a Thursday morning when there is a large market in the town – though the market is fun to visit, it makes it very difficult to park. Wet or cloudy days, when people are forced off the beaches in search of entertainment, see the longest queues.

To Cadaques

From Figueres it's about 30 km (18 miles) to **Cadaques**, a pretty fishing village made famous by Dalí. Nearby is Port Lligat, the tiny port where he and his wife Gala lived for many years in a house comprising several fishermen's cottages joined together, which has been open to the public since 1997.

As you drive down the hill towards the **Casa-Museu Dalí** you will see the Castor and Pollux heads and the large sculpted eggs on the roof – the

Right: the Teatre-Museu Dalí in Figueres

latter feature repeated on the Torre Galatea (mid-Jun–mid-Sep, daily 10.30am–9pm; mid-Sep–1 Nov and mid-Mar–mid-Jun, 10.30am–6pm, closed Mon; entrance fee; it is essential to book in advance because people are only allowed into the museum in small, carefully regulated groups; tel: 972 25 80 63). Set in a garden of gnarled olive trees, the house offers a wonderful insight into the unusual domestic life of the Dalís.

Huge windows frame views of the harbour and the Mediterranean, and in the Yellow Room a mirror is angled so that Dalí, in bed in the open-plan adjoining room, could see the light of the rising sun. Gala's touch is visible in many areas, particularly in the Room of the Cupboards where she covered cupboard doors with photos and magazine covers of special interest; and in the 'everlasting flowers' with which she festooned the windows.

The swimming pool area is a marvellous example of Dalían kitsch. The pool itself, modelled on one at the Alhambra in Granada, complete with fountains, shares space with a statue of Diana the Huntress and models of Michelin men and Pirelli tyres.

You could spend the night in the Hotel Port Lligat, almost next door to the house, where there's a pleasant restaurant and an excellent swimming pool (tel: 972 25 81 62), or in one of the small hotels in Cadaques.

The next day, return to Figueres where you can either take the motorway towards Girona, and turn onto the C-255 shortly before the city, or take a slower route on a pleasant side road (C-252 in the direction of the pottery town of La Bisbal) and look for signs to the **Castell Gala-Dalí** at Púbols (mid-Jun–mid-Sep, daily 10.30am–8pm; mid-Mar–mid-Jun and mid-Sep–1 Nov 10.30am–6pm, closed Mon; entrance fee).

Dalí restored this Gothic-Renaissance castle and gave it to Gala in 1970, promising only to enter it at her invitation. He painted frescoes in the interior and built the crypt where Gala is buried. He moved to the castle on the day of her death in 1982 and stayed, becoming increasingly frail, until a fire two years later obliged him to move to the Torre Galatea in Figueres.

4. THE HOLY MOUNTAIN *(see pull-out map)*

Montserrat, the serrated mountain, is Barcelona's most holy shrine. Its blunt, grey rocky walls rise to a sheer 1,241m (4,075ft) and extend over 50 sq km (18 sq miles) making it not only visible for miles around, but also easily identified on flights in and out of Barcelona airport.

Displayed in the 16th-century basilica of the monastic complex is the Black Virgin of Montserrat, **La Moreneta**, a Romanesque statue of the Madonna and Child that has been the subject of great veneration. Catalans are not especially known for their devoutness, and this statue and her mountain have captured their imagination for political as much as for religious reasons. In her rocky stronghold, La Moreneta is looked to for protection against invaders and tyrants. Her elected abbot is seen as an upholder of Catalan liberties. Catalans are expected to make a pilgrimage to this holy mountain once in their lives. Everything is spoken, sung and written only in Catalan.

Getting There

Montserrat lies 50km (30 miles) inland, 45 minutes by car along the new autovia to Martorell. Bus tours starting at 8–9am are organised by Julià, Sants Viriat Coach Station (tel: 93 317 64 54) and Pullmantur, Gran Via 635 (tel: 93 317 12 97). FGC trains run from Plaça Espanya from 9.30am. A cloudy or overcast day will ruin the wonderful views, and be warned that the weather at this height can be changeable, cold and turbulent.

The train follows the River Llobregat as far as the **Aeri de Montserrat** station, which it reaches in just over an hour. From here take the **cable car** up to the solid red-brick, institutional looking buildings of the monastery. In front of the Aeri station is the **Plaça de la Creu**, where the information office stands. The square gives the impression of a small town, with souvenir shops,

post office, bureau de change and restaurant. Head past the audio-visual building towards the **basilica**, reached through a 20th-century gateway. The monastery became a Benedictine establishment in AD967, but everything about it today is rather new. Its most recen destruction was in 1811 during the Napoleonic wars when, after a stout defence by Catalan guerillas, called *somatenes*, its treasures were plundered and its library burned. The monks did not return for more than 50 years and the basilica was given its present facade in 1900.

The abbey is open 6am–8pm, but the time to arrive is when the boys' choir, which has had a school here since the 13th century, sings (daily

Left: Casa-Museu Dalí at Port Lligat

1pm, 6.45pm; closed Jul and 26 Dec–8 Jan). Behind them, above the altar, is La Moreneta herself. There is a separate door at the front of the basilica for people wanting to see and touch this statue of Madonna and Child, blackened by centuries of candle smoke. The legend is that it was made by St Luke and brought to Barcelona by St Peter. All manner of royalty and nobility have pledged themselves to her. St Ignatius Loyola, founder of the Jesuits, dedicated himself to her service.

Outside the basilica in the Plaça de Santa Maria is the **museum** (9.30am–6pm daily), with ecclesiastical treasures and archaeology from Egypt, plus Roman and Byzantine ceramics. It also has a superb art collection, including works by El Greco, Caravaggio, Picasso, Dalí, Monet, Sisley and Degas.

The Way of the Cross

There are several excursions to be made from the monastery. The **Via Crucis**, the Way of the Cross, is behind the Plaça de l'Abat Oliba. Its modern statues lead to the hermitage of Sant Miquel. From Plaça de la Creu a cable car runs down to **Santa Cova**. This chapel is in a grotto where the Virgin is said to have been hidden during the Moorish occupation. But a clear day may demand a more spectacular excursion.

Sant Joan is one of the mountain's 13 small *ermitas* inhabited by hermits until Napoleon's troops, having hanged the monks, hunted them down 'like wild goats' and killed them.

Behind the funicular station in Plaça Santa Creu is another, which takes passengers up to the hermitage. There is a café and restaurant where it stops, then a 20-minute walk up to the hermitage. From here it is possible to walk to **Sant Jeroni**, the highest point of the mountain.

Anyone who stays longer than they intended might like to know that there are two places to stay in the monastery: the 2-star Hotel Monestir and the 3-star Abat Cisneros. For all information about Montserrat, tel: 93 877 77 01.

Above: the monastery at Montserrat. **Left:** La Moreneta
Right: the mountain road climbs steeply to the top

Leisure Activities

SHOPPING

Barcelona is an enormously attractive place to shop, from its innovative, designer-conscious showcases around Passeig de Gràcia and Diagonal to the bright lights of the port's Maremàgnum and the delightful little specialist shops that seem to have remained virtually unchanged for years in the sunless streets of the Barri Gòtic. Any shopping spree can be punctuated by sights of *Modernista* or Gothic architecture, and relieved by regular refreshment at pavement cafés or *tapes* bars.

Barcelona's fame has spread and people come a long way, especially with the prevailing favourable exchange rates, to buy fashionable clothes, leather bags and shoes; ceramics, especially earthenware, wickerwork, knives, scissors, stationery, perfumes, candles, dried flowers, lacework, antiques, prints and designer objects. That is to say nothing of the abundance of tempting and transportable food, from nuts and dried fruit to olives and virgin olive oil, available in markets and *colmados*, the wonderful old grocers' found in every neighbourhood.

Less attractive but ever-practical are the department stores and shopping centres: the long-established El Corte Inglés, with branches in Plaça Catalunya and Avinguda Diagonal and the latest one, specialising in music, books and sport, in Portal de l'Angel (open 10am–9.30pm), is the town's busiest department store.

Avinguda Portal de l'Angel is a lively shopping street, good for shoes and young fashion, running down from the Plaça Catalunya towards the cathedral, and turning into the equally lively Portaferrissa shopping street on the right at the bottom, which leads to La Rambla.

More fashionable and more fun than the department stores are the shopping malls. Bulevar Rosa was the first, in 1968, and remains one of the best (branches in Passeig de Gràcia and Diagonal). Gralla Hall in Portaferrissa is very hip. Relatively new are the huge shopping centres like El Triangle in Plaça Catalunya, which is known for its high-tech FNAC store, and L'Illa at Diagonal 545–57.

The latest and largest in Catalonia, La Maquinista, controversially replaced an enormous old factory in Sant Andreu (open from 10am–10pm). For late night shopping try VIPS in Rambla de Catalunya 7–9 with shops and cafés, or Maremàgnum in the harbour, where fashion shops are open until 11pm, when you can move straight into the discos. All these are stiff competition to Marks & Spencer, with branches now in Plaça Catalunya and L'Illa, favoured for their food more than anything else.

Eixample Chic
Designer clothes, designer furniture, designer stores… the Eixample is where the cutting edge of Barcelona's fashion lies, even though it is now being challenged by alternative movements in the Born and El Raval districts of the Old Town, where second-hand clothes and offbeat designs have become acceptable.

Left: a chic shop in the Eixample
Right: El Raval's new shopkeepers

Take the Eixample street by street: some shops are worth visiting just for window shopping and for a peek at their stylish interiors. Designer names to look out for include Antonio Miró, Josep Font, Armand Basi, David Valls, Lluís Generó and Purificación Garcia. Popular local chain stores include Massimo Dutti, Mango and the extremely successful Zara, the phenomenon of the nineties, where men, women and children can always find some solution to a clothing crisis.

Passeig de Gràcia: coming up from Plaça Catalunya, at No 4 is a revamped Gonzalo Comella, favoured by the up-town crowd, with their own and international labels; then for classic, stylish male fashion there's Furest at No 14, followed by Zara's flagship store in a spectacular building on the corner of Gran Via.

On the other side at No 35 is Loewe, for smart leatherware. Bulevar Rosa, the forerunner of Barcelona's malls, with some 70 shops, sells mostly fashion, and leather bags. At the Centre Català d'Artesania there are three rooms showing new local craft work. At No 89, Adolfo Dominguez, leading Spanish designer of classic fashion, has kitted out his own store. Just after Gaudí's La Pedrera, with an excellent souvenir shop, is Vinçon, the interior design store that is not to be missed.

Consell de Cent, just off Passeig de Gràcia, is the latest stylish domain of Barcelona's fashion king, Antonio Miró (no relation to the artist), something of a trailblazer in the late 1960s and still a leader. Men and women are both catered for.

Another street off this main avenue that is well worth checking out is Roselló, where Dos y Una at No 275, is an up market souvenir shop with creative gift ideas, like their Spanish bull pan scourer. At No 271, La Inmaculada Concepción specialises in all kinds of *Modernista* fixtures and fittings, and opposite is Z..Z..Vinçon, devoted to snoozing and bedrooms.

Rambla de Catalunya is full of interesting shopping possibilities and makes a pleasant walk. Muxart at No 47 is the subtlest shop front in a *Modernista* building, and sells very classy Catalan-designed shoes and bags. Or from the top of Passeig de Gràcia, you could go up Diagonal, where the shops become increasingly exclusive: at No 403, Pilma is a highly popular and sophisticated modern furniture shop that also sells wonderful objets d'art. No 466, Eleven, is a shoe shop with a striking modern interior designed by Manuel Ybarguengoitia and Maria del Mar Nogués.

Jean Pierre Bua at No 469, with a metal and concrete interior designed by Eduard Samsó, is where you will find all Spain's top designer names and international labels. Try No 598, Sara Navarra, for good, inexpensive shoes and leatherware, and keep on up for L'Illa.

Gothic Antiquities

There are some wonderful old shops in the Gothic quarter, and this is the best place to look for antiques and second-hand books as well as new fashion and interior design, and second-hand shops.

Behind the cathedral is a narrow street, Carrer Freneria, with Grafiques el Tinell at No 1, specialising in old prints and lithographs, especially posters of blocks of the old guild (*gremis*) trades and crafts usually seen in decorative tiles. Next door is La Caixa de Fang selling a fine range of earthenware. Around the corner at No 7 Llibreteria is an ancient candle shop, Cereria Subirà and walking towards Plaça Sant Jaume there's a colourful mixture of fashion and souvenir shops.

Cross the Plaça to Carrer del Call in the old Jewish quarter, where you'll find La Roda for earthenware and decorated ceramics and Obach for any kind of hat, especially a huge range of berets. This magnificent shop is on the corner of Banys Nous, where there are several attractive shops: at No 5 Gemma Povo stocks antiques including wrought iron, furniture and hand-blown glass, and Instinto has its own designs, stylish women's clothes in comfortable fabrics and jewellery. Germanes Garcia situated on the corner of Ave María is the best place to buy baskets and anything you could wish for in wicker, from desks to lampshades.

Plaça de Sant Josep Oriol: Molsa has ceramics ancient and modern, and Coses del Casa is good for fabrics. Carrer Petritxol, off Plaça del Pi, is full of jewellers and art galleries (Dalmau, who was Picasso and Miró's agent, operated from here). No 2, Libreria Quera, is the place to go for maps and photography books about the Catalan countryside. Plaça del Pi also has a little shop that sells a huge variety of comics

Shopping is a pleasant experience in the Born area where attractive small shops are opening constantly.

Markets

The big flea market is Els Encants in Plaça de les Glòries (Metro Line I). It's fun but most of it really is junk. It's held on Monday, Wednesday, Friday and Saturday from 8am–8pm; 7pm in winter.

An antique market is held in the cathe-

dral square (Thursday), and country produce is sold in the Plaça del Pi during the week. Painters sell their work in neighbouring Plaça Sant Josep Oriol at weekends. A stamp and coin market is held in the Plaça Reial from 9am–2.30pm on Sunday, worth visiting for the atmosphere.

Stamps, books and video games are on sale in Sant Antoni market from 9am–2pm on Sunday. The market is to the west of the Rambla at the far end of Carrer del Carme, continuing along Carrer de Sant Antoni Abat. Every weekend the lower part of La Rambla holds an arts and crafts fair, and on the other side of the Columbus monument is a bric-à-brac market.

Gifts and souvenirs

La Rambla is disappointing for shopping, apart from the newsstands, which are a feast of magazines and newspapers. Tacky souvenir shops sell Barça football memorabilia (which can also be bought at the Camp Nou's own shop), but one place, La Botiga de la Virreina, at No 99, makes up for them all with stylish goods and books, designed in or about Barcelona.

The attractive museum shops are another excellent source of gifts and temptation. The ones that particularly stand out are the shops at the Textile Museum, the history museums, and MACBA and CCCB.

Left: Els Encants flea market
Above: a comic shop in Plaça del Pi

EATING OUT

As in any civilised society, *barcelonins* are quite serious about their food. 'Where did you eat?' they will ask with uncharacteristic interest, and you know your reply will mark you out either as a person of taste and distinction or as someone who needs taking in hand. Catalan cuisine is an ancient Mediterranean cuisine, full of the aromas of mountain herbs, the oils and the juices of the plains, the wild meat of the woods and skies, and the flesh of the fish and crustaceans of the sea. *Mar i montanya* is how it is described, a special mixture of seafood and meat. The first cook book ever written in Europe was the Catalan *Llibre de Sant Sovi* of 1324.

Other cuisines can be tried in the city and there is no shortage of places to eat. The smarter restaurants tend to be in the Eixample or uptown, but they lack the personality of the old town where some great old establishments remain, for example Agut, Caracoles, Set Portes (*see below for some recommendations*) and alternative trendy places are opening.

Lunch is the best value, eaten from 2–4pm, when most restaurants have inexpensive three-course set menus with wine. An average à la carte may turn out to be twice the price. Dinner is eaten at about 10pm. Typically a meal will begin with an *amanida catalana*, a salad with cold meats; or *escalivada*, baked peppers and aubergines,

skinned, covered in oil and eaten cold; or *esqueixada*, a salad with shredded cod. A main course could be a *suquet*, fish stew or *estofat*, meat stew; or *botifarra amb mongetes*, sausage and beans; or rabbit, *conill*, served with snails (*cargols*) or with a garlicky *allioli* sauce. For dessert, *crema catalana*, a local *crème brulée*, is essential.

Alternatively, just a few portions *(racions)* or a smaller amount *(tapes)* can be filling, especially when eaten with a chunk of Catalonia's best invention, *pa amb tomàquet*, bread rubbed with garlic, fruity olive oil and tomato. Have it with ham (*pernil*), spicy sausage (*xoriço*), cheese (*formatge*) or anchovies (*anxoves*).

Other dishes to point to on the bar might include *truites,* omelettes made with potato and onion or with spinach; small fried fish; octopus; snails; or *patates braves*, potatoes in a hot tomato sauce.

Typical menu items
Entrants/Primer plat **Starter/First course**
Amanida **Green salad**
Empedrat **White bean salad with tomatoes, onions, salt cod, olives**
Espinacs a la catalana **Steamed spinach lightly fried with raisins and pine nuts**
Sopa de peix **Fish soup**
Gaspatxo **Andalucian cold tomato soup**
Escudella **Thick soup with noodles, the stock left from boiling meat**
Arros negre **Black rice, squid and its ink**

Above: eating outdoors on a warm summer evening

Cigrons **Chick peas, often stewed with chard** *(bledes),* **spinach, tiny clams or cod**
Llenties **Lentils, usually with spicy sausage and black pudding**
Faves a la catalana **Broad beans, stewed as lentils**
Verdures **Vegetable of the day, often overcooked with potatoes**
Canelons a la barcelonina **Cannelloni stuffed with meat**
Croquetes cassolanes **Home made croquettes (chicken, ham or salt cod)**

Segon plat **Main course**
Pollastre/Carn arrebossada
Chicken/meat (usually beef) fried in breadcrumbs
Peix (lluç, tonyina, gambes, sèpia…) a la planxa **Fish (hake, tuna, prawns, cuttlefish) cooked on a griddle. Meat or rabbit also cooked this way**
Calamars a la romana/farcits **Squid fried in batter/stuffed**
Mandonguilles **Meatballs**
Xai a la brasa **Lamb cooked on open wood or charcoal fire**
Fetge **Liver**
Pollastre rostit **Chicken roasted in a rich sauce**
Fricandó **Braised veal with wild mushrooms**
Salsitxes amb tomàquet **Thin sausages in tomato sauce**

Postres **Desserts**
Fruite (Poma, platan, pressec, sindria) **Fresh fruit (apple, banana, peach, watermelon etc)**
Macedonia **Fruit salad**
Flam **Crème caramel**
Postre de music **Nuts and dried fruits, often served with moscatel (sweet wine)**
Pastis **Tart/cake**
Gelat **Ice cream**
Mel i mató **Curd cheese with honey**

Where to Eat

Going for *tapes* can be a source of great fun in the **Barri Gòtic**, in the bars whose lights spill out on to the narrow medieval lanes. Carrer Mercè, behind Passeig de Colom has a good choice.

In the Eixample it is a smarter affair, with some traditional bars and modern *cervecerias* such as Tapa Tapa, Passeig de Gracia 44, where the tempting dishes line the bars. A new wave of Basque *tapes* bars are all over town. Try Irati, Cardenal Casanyas, 17, one of the first and best.

The **port** is a favourite area for eating, and there is no lack of restaurants along the quayside, particularly at the Palau de Mar, a good place for people-watching, and in Passeig Joan de Borbó. Salmonete in the **Maremàgnum** is the new site of the popular *chirringuito* restaurant that was torn down from the beach in Barceloneta. Others moved to the **Olympic Port**, where diners are spoilt for choice. Familiar names from Barceloneta, such as El Rey de la Gamba, jostle with new fish restaurants and of course the ubiquitous, cosmopolitan likes of Planet Hollywood.

Wines of the region are good, and unless you know what you are doing, stick to the house wine. Red is often served cold, which can improve the rougher stuff. White-wine drinkers might like to try the pinks *(rosat),* which can be very refreshing.

The Penedès wine region just to the south also produces champagne-method wines called *Cava,* which is a little more expensive than still wine. A small bottle of it, a *benjamin,* is a pleasant drink to have in a bar any time of day.

Recommendations

Many restaurants are closed on Sunday night and Monday, and some take an annual holiday in August. Even expensive restaurants offer good value set menus at lunch-time, or try a *menú de degustació,* a selection of their best food.

The Eixample *(Expensive)*
Botafumeiro
Carrer Gran de Gràcia, 81
Tel: 93 218 42 30
Frequently described as the greatest seafood place in town. Plus oyster bar. $$$

Jaume de Provença
Carrer de Provença, 88
Tel: 93 430 00 29
A cool, modern ambience is appropriate for one of Barcelona's leading *nouvelle cuisine* Catalan restaurants. $$$

Tragaluz
Passatge de la Concepció, 5
Tel: 93 487 01 96
Creative Mediterranean cuisine under large skylight. Spectacular Mariscal-designed loos. *Tapes* downstairs from 8.30pm. $$$

The Eixample *(Moderate)*
Casa Alfonso
Roger de Llúria, 6
Tel: 93 301 97 83
The restaurant in this well-established bar specialises in grilled meat, but the fun is eating Alfonso's excellent ham and other snacks at the bar. $$

El Japonés
Passatge de la Concepció, 2
Tel: 93 487 25 92
Trendy place for sushi. Stunning minimalist décor in this offspring of Tragaluz. $$

Madrid-Barcelona
Aragó, 282
Tel: 93 215 70 26
Renovating this classic old restaurant luckily didn't affect the bustling atmosphere or the good traditional dishes. Conveniently situated just off Passeig de Gràcia. $$

The Old Town *(Expensive)*
Agut d'Avignon
Carrer la Trinitat, 3
Tel: 93 302 60 34
Fashionable, sophisticated and lively. Catalan specialities. A good wine list. $$$

Amaya,
La Rambla, 20–24
Tel: 93 302 10 37
Big, lively and friendly with a good choice, particularly fish and Basque specialities. $$$

Casa Leopoldo
Carrer de Sant Rafael, 24
Tel: 93 441 30 14
A family run classic in the narrow streets of the barri Xines, renowned for its fish. $$$

Can Majó
Carrer d'Almirall Aixada, 23
Tel: 93 221 54 55
One of the best and most established fish restaurants in the newly revitalised Barceloneta area. Good paella. $$$

Gran Café
Carrer d'Avinyó, 9
Tel: 93 318 79 86
Smart, nostalgic decor, in a grand old former sewing-machine shop. $$$

Set Portes
Passeig d'Isabel II, 14
Tel: 93 319 30 33
Many well-known names have dined here over the years, including Picasso and Lorca. Founded in 1836, it's a Barcelona institution and a worthy one. Seafood and rice dishes are its specialities. $$$

The Old Town *(Moderate)*
Cafè de L'Acadèmia
Lledó 1
Tel: 93 315 00 26
Refreshingly different Catalan dishes in pleasant surroundings, with candle-lit outdoor tables set in a Gothic square. $$

Can Lluís
Carrer Cera, 49
Tel: 93 441 60 81
Out of the way and intimate, this little restaurant serves good local food. $$

Els Quatre Gats
Montsió, 3
Tel: 93 302 41 40
The café Puig i Cadafalch built and which the artists frequented has been restored, and though maybe not the best food in town, it's fun to sit where they all sat. $$

Estrella de Plata
Pla del Palau 9,
Tel: 93 319 60 07

Left: *esqueixada* is a Catalan speciality

Local joint transformed into a creative *tapes* bar, using the best ingredients. Excellent house wine. $$

Los Caracoles
Carrer dels Escudellers, 14
Tel: 93 302 31 85
Another institution. This has just the kind of atmosphere one imagines an old Barcelona restaurant should have. Popular with tourists, but well worth a visit. $$

Rita Blue
Plaça de Sant Agustí, 3
Tel: 93 412 34 38
The local saint of the impossible has given her name to this fun, trendy bar/restaurant with excellent fusion food. $$

Santa María
Carrer del Comerç, 17
Tel: 93 315 12 27
Serving new-generation Catalan food in delicate amounts, this attractive small restaurant has become very trendy. Delicious, exciting flavours. $$

Senyor Parellada
Argenteria, 37,
Tel: 93 310 50 94
Stylish brasserie with great atmosphere; new and traditional Catalan dishes. $$

Taxidermista
Plaça Reial, 8
Tel: 93 412 45 36
Snacky Mediterranean food in this good-looking café-cum-restaurant, named after its former owner's occupation. $$

The Old Town *(Inexpensive)*
Egipte
La Rambla, 79
Tel: 93 317 74 80
A great bistro-type place with tasty value-for-money dishes in antique-filled rooms. $

El Portalón
Banys Nous, 20
Tel: 93 302 11 87
Good value *menú del día,* pitchers of rough red wine and locals playing dominoes. A gem. Winter bean stews especially good. $

La Cassola
Carrer de Sant Sever, 3
Tel: 93 318 15 80
Welcoming family-run restaurant with good home cooking and Catalan specialities. $

La Dolça Herminia
Magdalenes 27
Tel: 93 317 06 76
Unusual dishes in a surprisingly reasonable fixed menu amid soothing, sophisticated décor, just off the busy Via Laietana. $

Lluna Plena
Carrer Montcada, 2
Tel: 93 315 17 29
Near the Picasso Museum. Good, inexpensive food in attractive surroundings. $

Other districts *(Moderate)*
Agua
Passeig Marítim, 30
Olympic Village
Tel: 93 225 12 72
Just beneath the giant goldfish, one of the few stylish places serving good food on the beach. Sought-after, so book. $

Casa Joana
Major de Sarrià, 59
Sarrià
Tel: 93 203 10 36
Checked tablecloths and home cooking (delicious *canelons* and braised veal) in this old 'village' restaurant. $

Above: Els Quatre Gats

NIGHTLIFE

'One morning I was awakened at four by loud conversation; going out on my balcony and looking down, I perceived that the rambla was still full of people sitting at café tables or on seats beneath trees, or strolling to and fro, talking, laughing and screaming with the greatest vivacity, the street lights that gleamed above the plane trees now paling a little in a faint dawn… It was a pretty and fantastic sight, this crowd bewitched into perpetual nocturnal animation.'

Rose Macaulay was writing in 1949, and though the Rambla today is not like that every night, *barcelonins*, like all Spaniards,

have an extraordinary capacity to stay up late. The working day doesn't end until 8pm, which means that nobody sits down to eat until around 10pm, so most entertainments don't begin until after that.

Nightclubs warm up from 2am and when they close around 5am people move on to *Afters*, bars that stay open till mid-morning. The real die-hards find places they can dance all day long, but it can cause havoc to your work schedule. The late-night crowds build up from Thursday through to Saturday.

Concerts, theatre, cinema
The main classical music venues are the **Palau de la Música Catalana**, the new **Au-**

ditori and the refurbished **Gran Teatre del Liceu** on the Rambla. Watch out for music played in other imposing surroundings, such as the **Saló de Cent** in the town hall; **Sant Felip Neri** and **Santa María del Pi** in the Gothic quarter and **Santa María del Mar**, where jazz is also sometimes played.

In the summer there's often music in public parks and medieval squares. From July to September musical evenings are held on the atmospheric roof terrace of Gaudí's La Pedrera and the Fundació Joan Miró has a summer season of contemporary music.

The principle theatres are the **National Theatre** (TNC) near Plaça de les Glòries Catalanes; **Poliorama**, Rambla 15; the picturesque **Tivoli**, which often has modern, international productions in its early 20th century décor; and the **Mercat de les Flors**, Carrer de Lleida 19, with various spaces. The **Teatre Malic**, Fussina 3, is a tiny basement theatre that always has an interesting programme, as does the nearby **Espai Escènic Joan Brossa**.

Original-language (V.O.) films are shown at various cinemas, including **Casablanca** (Passeig de Gràcia,115); **Renoir- Les Corts**, Eugeni d'Ors 12, is a bit out of the way but shows good films on six screens; the **Icaria Yelmo** in the Olympic Village has 15 screens, and just about every film you could hope for; and the **Verdi** complex with 9 screens in Gràcia (Carrer Verdi, 32) is also a great place for a drink or snack afterwards. Remember that most films don't start until around 10pm

There are regular rock concerts, open-air in the Olympic Stadium or inside the impressive Palau Sant Jordi and all over town at festival time. More intimate concerts take place in **Bikini** (Déu i Mata, 105), **La Boîte**, a former jazz club (Av. Diagonal, 447) and **Zeleste** in Poble Nou (Almogàveres, 122). In the Grec summer arts festival, music features strongly. There is a Jazz Festival in the Autumn and a Festival of Ancient Music in April and May. Keep an eye on local listings for the latest.

Bars, clubs and discos
Every night from pre-dinner cocktail hour until dawn, bar-flies hop from one nightspot to another all over town. In competing for

Above: audience participation in a Paral.lel nightclub

custom, bars offer an enormous variety of ambiences and styles, with various cocktails of music and drink. The smoother, designer bars tend to be in uptown Eixample, like the cool **Nick Havanna** (Carrer Rosselló 208) – the original designer bar from the 1980s – or **Snooker** (Roger de Llúria, 42), where you can have a game if you wish.

However, it is downtown Barri Gòtic that has become the place for the young and trendy, though it does have a range to suit all tastes: from traditional old bars such as **Portalón** (Carrer Banys Nous, 20) where the wine comes from barrels to the classic cocktail bar **Boadas** (Tallers, 1). The daughter of its founder still shakes a mean Dry Martini. In the narrow streets between the Plaça George Orwell and the Plaça Reial, a new 'latest bar' opens every other month, from grunge to 1970s vinyl to cool lounge bars. **Al Limón Negro** (Escudellers Blancs) is an example, as is **Oviso** (Pl. George Orwell), which has a popular terrace. In La Ribera, **El Born** (Passeig del Born, 26) in an old fish store, is just one of many places mushrooming in the labyrinth of medieval streets. **El Xampanyet**, serving its own *Cava* in Carrer de Montcada is worth a detour, though visitors to the Picasso museum will have got there first. Jazz fans might head for the **London Bar** (Nou de la Rambla, 34), the **Jamboree** (Plaça Reial), or the **Harlem** (Comtessa de Sobradiel).

Nightclubs differ from bars in that they have an entrance fee (which will probably include the first drink). Again, they range from traditional discos to dance spaces with in-house or imported DJs to classic dance halls. In **La Paloma** (Tigre 27) local couples dance regularly at afternoon sessions, as they have for the past 50 years, an experience not to be missed. Later on the band do salsa and after 3am the DJs move in with a hip new crowd. The **Torres de Avila** in the Poble Espanyol is visited for its design by Mariscal and Arribas more than its atmosphere.

Toilets are a point of style: at **Velvet** (Carrer de Balmes 161) men use a huge trough; at **Rosebud** in Tibidabo the doors to the men's and women's lead to the same place. Other wild spots include, **Satanassa** (Carrer d'Aribau 27) and **Moog** (Arc del Teatre, 3) for dance.

Nightclubs and discos are usually quiet until well after midnight (although if you don't follow the crowd you might get the idea that some of them never get going at all). **KGB** in Carrer d'Alegre de Dalt 55 is a long-standing favourite, as is **Otto Zutz**, Carrer de Lincoln 15, one of the original designer discos that sometimes has live music. A new night spot for cool drinks and dancing is Maremàgnum in the middle of the harbour, where there's a selection of good bars and discos.

When the party's finally over a dawn breakfast of chocolate and *churros* is inviting, at somewhere like **Vall d'Ouro**, Carrer Paris 198, off the Diagonal. It serves breakfast from 5am.

Flamenco, not a Catalan dance, has been increasing in popularity recently. A typical place to see it is **El Patio Andaluz** (Carrer d'Aribau, 242; dinner or drink and show), or **Los Tarantos** (Plaça Reial, 17). For cabaret acts delve into the Barri Xinés, between La Rambla and along Paral.lel, still, but only just, the seedy part of town.

There are still a few music halls left, like the **Arnau** (Paral.lel, 60) or **Barcelona City Hall** (Rambla de Catalunya, 2–4º). The **Apolo** (Nou de la Rambla 113) has become a trendy club with dance music and live concerts. And for those who want a flutter the **Gran Casino de Barcelona** is now in the Olympic port, a far cry from the trendy night life in the Old Town.

Right: getting in the party mood

CALENDAR OF EVENTS

'The Catalans are the best innkeepers in Spain, and among the least bad cooks; and, although rude, unsocial and unfriendly to strangers, the Barcelonese among themselves are fond of gaity, feasting and masking.' The English travel writer Richard Ford never let courtesy muddy his prose.

'Masquerading is almost of absolute necessity to Spaniards,' he went on in his 1845 *Handbook for Travellers to Spain*, 'and especially to the intelligent Catalonians, whose capital is the head-quarters of the mask.'

The people of Barcelona today still like feasting and masking. These are wild and boisterous, but not usually drunken, occasions. Celebrations are held on the eve of the feasts, and last till dawn. The larger ones go on for several days.

Under Franco's dictatorship, pre-Lent **carnival** was banned in Catalonia from 1936 to 1980 but has since resurfaced as a spectacular event, most particularly in Sitges, a small town just south of the city, where a solid gay contingent in the processions always draws great applause.

At carnival straight men often dress as

women, too, and masked balls are held all over the town. If you are in Barcelona's Boqueria market (on the Rambla) at carnival time you will see stallholders entering into the spirit of the occasion, wearing masks or costumes as they serve their customers.

After carnival things are relatively quiet until the explosive celebration on the eve of the Feast of St John, **Sant Joan**, on 24 June. As in many other countries in Europe this is traditionally a night of midsummer bonfires, an ancient ritual with pagan origins that was adopted and adapted by the Christian church.

In Barcelona and the rest of Catalonia it is particularly joyous and greeted as the beginning of summer, even though the weather has warmed up before then. For several days leading up to it little boys throw fireworks annoyingly about the streets, and though there are some beautiful firework displays on the night, it can also be deafening. *Cava* is drunk and *coca* bread is eaten.

Each local quarter, or *barri*, has its own festival; some are confined to a street, others to wider areas. One of the best and most atmospheric is in the **Gràcia** *barri*. This one lasts for a week in August when the city is otherwise quite quiet. It attracts some good bands as well as turning out its *drac* (dragon), *gegants* (giants) and *dimonis* (devils).

However, the fiesta to end all fiestas is Barcelona's own **Festa Major** centred around the city's patron saint, La Mercè, whose winged figure flies on the skyline over her church behind the Passeig de Colom. Her feast day is on 24 September and in the **Setmana Gran** (the Big Week) there is a whole week of masking, dancing and feasting, with particularly fiery dragons and devils chasing people through the streets, the whole thing culminating in firework displays and bonfires.

Nationalist festivals

The more sober nationalist festivals are times for putting out the red-and-yellow striped Catalan flag. St George is Catalonia's patron saint and on his day, **Sant Jordi**, 23 April, bookstalls are set up in the Plaça Sant Jaume and throughout the city. Alongside them, single red roses are sold to men and boys who do not seem the least embarrassed

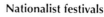

Left: the *castellers'* human towers are an integral part of many festivals

to buy them and carry them home through the streets for their mothers, girlfriends, mistresses and wives.

The book connection has less to do with St George than with the fact that 23 April is the anniversary of the death (in 1616) of Miguel de Cervantes (author of *Don Quixote*). William Shakespeare was born and died on the same date, and it has now been named World Book Day, in honour of the two great men.

The **Diada de Catalunya** on 11 September is an extremely sober occasion. This is the national day that commemorates the banning of the Catalan language and the loss of many ancient rights to Madrid, after troops led by the Bourbon king Felipe V captured Barcelona in 1713 following a devastating 13-month siege.

For obvious political reasons, the Diada was banned under Franco's regime but re-emerged after his death as a day of demonstrations and political activity.

Religious festivals are not celebrated here as elaborately as in many other parts of Spain. Christmas is preceded by the **Santa Llúcia** fair around the cathedral, selling decorations, gifts and everything you need to set the nativity scene. On a crisp winter day, with the smell of roast chestnuts in the air, it's a most enjoyable and festive occasion.

Christmas day itself is a family affair with a big get-together and blow-out meals on Boxing Day. New Year is celebrated with parties and dances, much as it is elsewhere in Europe. One national custom is to eat a grape and drink a sip of champagne on every stroke of the midnight hour, to ensure good luck throughout the year. Children look forward to the Three Kings, **Reis Mags**, on 6 January (Epiphany), for this is the day they customarily receive their presents. The kings arrive in the port by boat and tour the streets giving out sweets.

Easter is heralded by religious processions during Holy Week, albeit far less devout than they used to be – and still are in some parts of Spain. Children only have a few days' holiday from school, and many people use the long weekend to get out of the city to the coast and the countryside.

The major festivals will have dancing giants and some will also have *castellers*, human towers that try to break records as the crowd pushes them onwards and upwards. There will also, more often than not, be a *sardana*, Catalonia's national dance, in which people hold hands in replicating circles. The 11-man band, called a *cobla*, plays on brass and wind instruments. They can otherwise be seen and heard outside the cathedral at noon on Sunday.

Above: giants in the Plaça Sant Jaume on the feast of La Mercè

Practical Information

GETTING THERE

By Air

Barcelona airport (tel: 93 298 38 38) is about 12km (7 miles) south of the city at El Prat. Iberia is the country's national carrier and there is a shuttle service from here to the capital, Madrid.

The airport is equipped with tourist offices, banks, car-hire facilities and a hotel reservation service. Trains leave for the city every 30 minutes for Sants (about 20 minutes). There are also trains to Plaça Catalunya and Arc de Triomf. The excellent Aerobus leaves for Plaça Catalunya every 15 minutes.

The main airlines have offices in the city. Iberia's office is at Diputació, 258; tel: 93 401 33 81. For international reservations, tel: 93 412 47 48.

By Road

The French border is 149km (92 miles) north at La Jonquera on the A7 motorway. The toll amounts to around 1,500 pesetas. Avoid Friday night and Sunday evening rush-hours. The Royal Automobile Club of Catalunya (RACC) is manned 24 hours. It is at Avinguda Diagonal, 687, Barcelona 08028; tel: 93 495 50 00/900 365 505 (244).

By Rail

The main RENFE stations are Estació de França which is by the port, and Sants, which is towards the south. But many trains go through the city. If they do, it may well be more convenient to disembark at Passeig de Gràcia or Plaça de Catalunya. For all rail enquiries, tel: 93 490 11 22 (national), 902 24 02 02 (international).

By Sea

Trasmediterranea has a regular ferry service to the Balearic islands. For bookings, tel: 902 454645. The Buquebus is a fast ferry to Palma, tel: 93 44 97 74.

Left: getting a great view of the city

When to Go

Average winter temperatures are 54°F (12°C), summers 75°F (24°C). Winter evenings can be chilly but the sun can shine, too. Easter and autumn are mild and pleasant. Schools break up for the summer around 24 June and by August the city is so humid that some 60 percent of businesses close down for the month, which makes it delightfully empty, but also sometimes frustrating. People dress well in the city, whatever the weather.

TRAVEL ESSENTIALS

Passports

Passports are required by all non-Spaniards. It's a good idea to have a photocopy of the relevant pages, which usually do for ID and save taking the real thing everywhere.

Tourist Offices abroad:

Australia: Level 2
203 Castlereagh Street
PO Box A-685
Sydney NSW 2000
Tel: 2 9264 7966; fax: 2 9267 5111.

Canada: 34th Floor
2 Bloor Street West
Toronto
Ontario M4W 3E2.
Tel: 416 961 3131; fax: 416 961 1992

UK: 22–23 Manchester Square
London W1M 5AP.
Tel: 0207 486 8077; fax: 0207 486 8034

USA: Floor 35
666 Fifth Avenue
New York, NY 10103
Tel: 212 265 8822; fax: 212 265 88 64.

Consulates in Barcelona

Australia	tel: 93 330 94 96
Canada	tel: 93 215 07 04
Ireland	tel: 93 491 50 21
UK	tel: 93 419 90 44
USA	tel: 93 280 22 27

Health

There are no hidden health hazards. Water is drinkable but can taste unpleasant because of the purifying salts used. Mineral water is readily available (*agua con gas* is sparkling, *sin gas* is still). A chemist (*farmàcia*) is the best place to go with minor ailments. For UK citizens a form E111 is supposed to reciprocate health facilities within the EU, but private insurance is safer and is recommended.

Time Zones

Spain is one hour ahead of Greenwich Mean Time (Eastern Standard Time + 6 hrs) in winter; two in summer.

USEFUL INFORMATION

Money

The cost of living is similar to most other European countries. The currency is the euro (€). Traveller's cheques are widely accepted. Bank hours are usually 8.30am–2pm Monday to Friday. Major credit cards are accepted and most banks have cash points. For American Express tel: 91 572 03 03; Visa 900 991 216; MasterCard 900 971 1231.

Business Hours

Hours vary, but generally most shops and businesses open 9am–2pm and 4–8pm. Many public bodies work straight through from 8am–3pm, a particularly popular work schedule in summer.

Holidays

The city closes down on public holidays and many people leave town, particularly if they can snatch another day – known as a *puente*, or bridge – between the day off and the weekend. Christmas is not such an occasion as it is in northern Europe and school holidays then, and at Easter, are short.

1 January	New Year
6 January	Epiphany/Els Reis
19 March	Sant Josep
Good Friday	
Easter Monday	
Pascua Granada	
24 June	Sant Joan, Midsummer's Day
15 August	Feast of the Assumption
11 September	La Diada: Catalan National Day
24 September	La Mercè festival
12 October	Hispanitat, Spanish National Day
1 November	All Saints
6 December	Constitució, Constitution Day
8 December	Immaculate Conception
25 December	Christmas Day
26 December	St Stephen's Day

Religious Services

Catholic: Paroisse Françoise (in French and English), Anglí 15, tel: 93 204 49 62. **Anglican:** St George's Church, Sant Joan de la Salle, 41, tel: 93 417 88 67. **Jewish:** Sinagoga de la Comunidad Judia, Avenir 24, tel: 93 200 61 48. **Islamic:** Toarek Ben Ziad, Hospital 91, tel: 93 441 91 49.

LANGUAGE

Although Catalan is the local language, so many people from other parts of Spain live in Barcelona too that Castilian (Spanish) is also useful. Here are some helpful phrases:

English	Catalan/Spanish
Good morning	Bon dia/ Buenos dias
Good afternoon	Bona tarda/ Buenas tardes

EMERGENCIES

Crime

In any city, tourists are a target for pick-pockets and muggers. Only carry what you are likely to need. Never leave valuables in your car, always wear cameras and bags with their straps securely across your chest, and avoid the narrow Old Town streets at night.

In case of theft, assault or loss contact the National (091) or City (092) police. It is essential that you make a statement *(denuncia)* at a police station (e.g. in Nou de la Rambla, 80 or in the metro of Plaça Catalunya) in case of passport loss or to make an insurance claim. There is a 24-hour, multilingual tourist assistance scheme run by the Guardia Urbana at No 43 in La Rambla (tel: 93 301 90 60).

Medical Help

In cases of emergency go directly to the *urgències* (accident) departments at any of these hospitals: Hospital Sant Pau, Carrer Sant Antoni María Claret 167 (tel: 436 47 11), or Hospital Clínic, Carrer Villarroel, 170 (tel: 93 227 54 00).

Dentist: Clínica Janos, Carrer de Muntaner 375 6º 2ª, (tel: 93 200 23 33). Open daily 8am–1.30pm, 4–8.30pm. Institut Dexeus, Passeig de Bonanova 67 (tel: 93 212 75 36). Open daily 9am–9pm.

Emergency Numbers

General: 112
Fire Brigade: 080
Ambulance Service: 061
Tourist Police: 93 301 90 60
Lost Property: 93 402 31 61

COMMUNICATIONS & MEDIA

Telephone

Phone booths take coins and phone cards (available at *estancos* or post offices), with the latter being the most suitable for calls abroad. Some phone booth also take credit cards. It can be easier to phone first and pay later in one of the privately run telephone exchanges. However, beware of the bill, as rates are high.

Good night:	Bona nit/ Buenas noches
Goodbye	Adeu/Adios
Please	Si us plau/ Por favor
Thank you	Gracies/ Gracias
Where is…?	On es…?/ Donde esta…?
How much is it?	Quant val?/ Cuanto es?
one	un(a)/uno
two	dos (dues)/dos
three	tres/tres
four	quatre/cuatro
five	cinc/cinco
six	sis/seis
seven	set/siete
eight	vuit/ocho
nine	nou/nueve
ten	deu/diez
Do you have a room for night?	Té una habitació per una nit/Tiene una habitación para una noche?
Open	Obert/Abierto
Closed	Tancat/Cerrado
Today	Avui/Hoy
Tomorrow	Demà/Mañana
Yesterday	Ahir/Ayer

Left: there are plenty of opportunities to change money in the city
Above: Barcelona's distinctive phone boxes are usually in good working order

To dial Barcelona from abroad use the code for Spain (34) followed by that for Barcelona (93). From anywhere in Spain and in the city itself, Barcelona numbers begin with 93. From Barcelona, the international operator service for Europe is 1008, for the rest of the world 1005.

To call other countries, first dial the international access code 00, then the relevant country code: Australia (61); France (33); Germany (49); Italy (39); Japan (81); Netherlands (31); UK (44); US and Canada (1). If you are using a credit phone card, dial the company's access number below, then 01, and then the country code. AT&T, tel: 900 99 00 11; Interglobe, tel: 900 97 44 79; MCI, tel: 900 99 00 14; Sprint, tel: 900 99 00 13.

Post Offices

The main post office is in Plaça Antoni Lopez near the port, open 9am–9pm Monday to Friday, 9am–2pm Saturday. Other post offices *(correu)* are open in the mornings only. Stamps can be bought at tobacconists *(tabacs)*, which have brown and yellow signs.

Internet Connections

There are no end of places now available for checking your e-mail: on La Rambla and off it, in hotels and in cafés. For example: El Café de Internet Gran Vía de les Corts Catalanes, 656, tel: 93 412 19 15. 9am–midnight, from 10am on Saturday. Closed Sunday. www.cafeinternet.es

This cafe has a good atmosphere with a bar downstairs where a reasonable fixed lunch menu is available. This was the first to open.

Or there's easyEverything Ronda Universitat 35, another star product from the Easy family promising the fastest Internet connections. Open 24 hours, 7 days a week, with 300 computers. There's not much of a refreshment service, but still they're queuing. More are due to open.

Media

Barcelona's daily papers are *La Vanguardia*, *El Periodico* (published in Spanish and Catalan) and *Avui* (Catalan). The national *El Pais* has a Barcelona edition. All of them cover events in the city. *Guía del Ocio* is the local weekly listings magazine, with good coverage of what's on in town. *Metropolitan*, a useful free English monthly is available in the Palau de la Virreina (La Rambla, 99) and from some bars and bookshops.

GETTING AROUND

A car is unnecessary in Barcelona, which has buses and a good Metro system. A map of the city is essential. These are supplied by the tourist offices, who continually update their information pamphlets covering the city's culture and sites.

Tourist Information Offices

The main Barcelona tourist office is beneath Plaça Catalunya (near Portal del Angel; 9am–9pm daily). It's fully equipped with exchange facilities, hotel booking and internet services.

Other tourist offices are to be found in Sants Station (8am–8pm, winter weekends 8am–2pm); in the Town Hall (Plaça Sant Jaume; 10am–8pm; Sunday 10am–2pm; www.bcn.es); and at Barcelona airport (9am–7pm; Saturday 9am–2pm; closed Sunday; Terminal A, tel: 93 478 47 04; Terminal B, tel: 93 478 05 65).

For tourist information on Catalonia go to Palau Robert, Passeig de Gràcia, 107 (10am–7pm; Sunday 10am–2pm; tel: 93 238 40 00; www.gencat.es/probert).

Left Luggage

There are left luggage lockers at França, Sants and Passeig de Gràcia stations and at the Maritime station on the Moll de

Left: catching up with the news at a newsstand on La Rambla

Barcelona. There is also storage in the Barcelona Nord bus station.

Metro
There are five colour-coded Metro lines, which are numbered 1–5. Tickets are inexpensive and it's worth buying a T-1 card (to get 10 journeys for the price of five and a half), which can also be used on the buses and FGC line.

FGC
Ferrocarrils de la Generalitat de Catalunya (FGC) are similar to the Metro but extend inland to Sarrià, Tibidabo, Reina Elisenda and the other stops up towards the Collserola hills. They run from Plaça Catalunya, and go beyond the hill to Terrassa and Sabadell. The FGC line at Plaça d'Espanya goes to Manresa and Igualada and stops close to Montserrat mountain.

Bus
Bus lanes make journeys nearly as swift as the Metro. All night services (Nitbus) pass through Plaça Catalunya.

Taxi
The distinctive black-and-yellow Barcelona taxis are not expensive. The standard fare, which varies according to the time of day and whether it's a weekend or not, is set by the meter. A small tip is always appreciated. Luggage costs extra.

CITY PARKS

The *espais urbans* (urban spaces) are planned havens scattered around the city: for example, in front of the main RENFE station Sants (Metro lines 3 and 5), is the Plaça Països Catalans, and nearby is the much-photographed **Parc de l'Espanya Industrial**, which was designed by the Basque architect Luis Peña Ganchegui on the site of a former textile factory. Centred on a large lake where rowing boats can be hired, the 5-ha (12-acre) space is dominated by 10 futuristic watch towers.

The **Parc Joan Miró**, in Carrer d'Aragó, is well signposted by the artist's towering 22-m (70-ft) colourful mosaic-covered sculpture *Dona i Ocell* (Woman and Bird). The park is on two levels and occupies a former slaughterhouse, which gives it its other name, Parc de l'Escorxador. The sculpture rises from a small pond in the upper level; the lower level has palm-lined avenues brightened by oleander.

Formal gardens are not generally a feature of the city, but one pleasant example is the **Parc del Laberint de Horta** located behind the Velòdrom cycle track in the Vall d'Hebron, on the northwestern edge of the city and set against the heights of the Serra de Collserola.

The Velòdrom is on the inland side of the Passeig de la Vall d'Hebron, part of the city's new ring road, 10 minutes' walk up from

Above: ascending Tibidabo by funicular

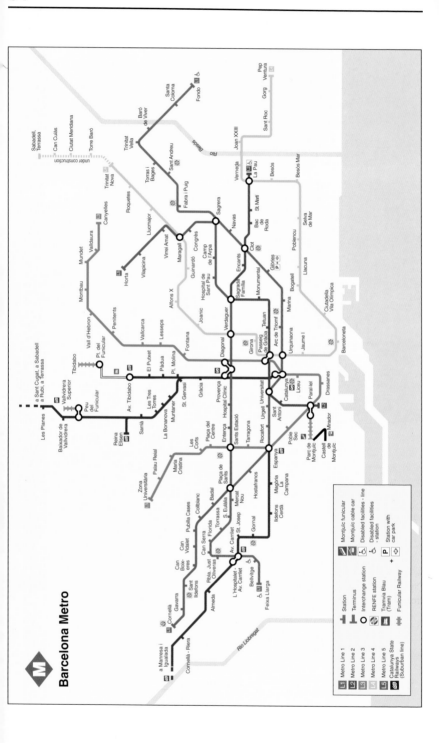

Barcelona Metro

practical information

ACCOMMODATION

There is a wide choice of good hotels in the city, and more are being built all the time. It is essential to book in advance, not just during the tourist season, but any time of year, on account of the number of trade fairs and conventions that are held in the city, as well as increasing tourism.

Prices range from around 150–270 euro for a double room in a five-star hotel to approximately 35–45 euro in a pleasant small hotel: however, the star system is not necessarily an accurate indication of price. In general, the more modestly priced hotels and hostels are situated downtown. Head for the streets off the Rambla if you are looking for bargain *pensions*.

In the Eixample
Avenida Palace★★★★
Gran Via de les Corts Catalanes 605, 08007
Tel: 93 301 96 00
Fax: 93 318 12 34
This is an old-fashioned gilded palace which was formerly a cinema, and is frequently recommended.

Claris Gran Luxe★★★★
Pau Claris 150, 08009
Tel: 93 487 62 62
Fax: 93 215 79 70
Latter-day luxuries and ancient art in the smooth modern interior built behind the façade of the 19th-century Palau Vedruna, where you can even rent 'house' mopeds to whiz around town.

Condes de Barcelona★★★★
Passeig de Gràcia 75, 08008
Tel: 93 484 22 00
Fax: 93 484 21 90
Occupying an attractive *Modernista* building, the Condes de Barcelona has great character and is set in a wonderful location.

Duques de Bergara★★★★
Carrer de Bergara 11, 08002
Tel: 93 301 51 51
Fax: 93 317 34 42
Located just off Plaça de Catalunya, this hotel occupies a fine *fin-de-siècle* mansion and has a delightfully personal atmosphere.

Montbau, on Metro line 3. It is easily identified by the gas spheres up above it, which look very similar to two great eyeballs keeping watch over the city. On the far side a footbridge has been incorporated to take pedestrians directly to the Laberint park. The whole place is the inspiration of the Marqués of Alfarres, who early last century had a neo-Islamic mansion built around a medieval tower.

To the right of it, approached from the rear, is the attractive walled **Patí de les Carmelites** (10am–2pm daily) offering topiaried walks, yuccas and tall palms.

Nearby, and entirely different in style is the **Parc de la Creueta del Coll**. Two stops back down the Metro line at Penitents, just below the sports complex built for the Olympics, this bright new public space was created in a disused quarry by Joan Martorell and David Mackay, two local architects. Among its various attractions is an outdoor swimming pool complete with a sandy beach and the *Elogi de l'Agua* (Water Eulogy) sculpture by Eduardo Chillida suspended overhead.

The third park in this area, just below the Creueta del Coll, is perhaps the best known of Barcelona's parks because of its *Modernista* architect: this is Gaudí's **Park Güell** (*see Itinerary 3, page 34*).

Above: the Old Town is the best bet for inexpensive accommodation

Gallery★★★★

Carrer Rosselló 249, 08008
Tel: 93 415 99 11
Fax: 93 415 91 84
In heart of the Eixample with all mod cons, this efficient but friendly hotel has the added bonus of a peaceful and attractive garden at the rear. Request a room looking on to it when you make your reservation.

Gran Hotel Havana★★★★

Gran Via de les Corts Catalanes 647, 08010
Tel: 93 412 11 15
Fax: 93 412 26 11
The Gran Hotel Havana has a serene and elegant modern interior behind a traditional Eixample facade, filled with light from a spectacular glass atrium. The rooms are pleasant if rather on the small side, and the staff are affable.

Majestic★★★★

Passeig de Gràcia 70, 08007
Tel: 93 488 17 17
Fax: 93 488 18 80
This large hotel, which was thoroughly re-vamped in 1999, is now extremely sophis-ticated and has two highly recommended restaurants.

Granvia★★★

Gran Via de les Corts Catalanes 642, 08007
Tel: 93 318 19 00
Fax: 93 318 99 97
This older-style hotel has a great location close to the Passeig de Gràcia and offers plenty of personality. It also represents ex-cellent value. -

Neutral★★

Rambla de Catalunya 42, 08007
Tel: 93 487 63 90
Fax: 93 487 40 28
Comfortable hotel which offers reasonable value. For great views, ask for a balcony overlooking the street.

Windsor★★

Rambla de Catalunya 84, 08008
Tel: 93 215 11 98
Bright, clean and very well situated.

Hostal Ciudad Condal

Carrer Mallorca 255, 08008
Tel: 93 215 10 40
Shortcomings in interior décor easily com-pensated by central location in this accept-able, well-positioned *pension*.

San Medin

Gran de Gràcia 125, 08012
Tel: 93 217 30 68
A comfortable little *pension* at the top end of the Passeig de Gràcia.

Seafront and Ciutadella

Arts Hotel★★★★

Passeig de la Marina 19
Tel: 93 221 10 00
Fax: 93 221 10 70
A high-rise hotel with a very high profile, it stands by the beach and marks the entrance to the Olympic Village. Every comfort plus panoramic views.

Park★★★

Avinguda Marquès de l'Argentera 11, 08003
Tel: 93 319 60 00
Fax: 93 319 45 19
Wonderful period-piece from the 1950s, carefully restored in 1990, this is a great ho-tel, ideal for El Born nightlife and access to beach. Very good value.

Triunfo★★

Passeig de Picasso 22
Tel: 93 315 08 60
Fax: 93 315 08 60
The Triunfo is a simple, basic but very clean little *pension* situated, like the Park Hotel, conveniently close to Ciutadella and El Born's attractions

Above: the Hotel Suizo has a tempting *pasteleria* next door

The Old Town

Le Meridien★★★★
Rambla 111, 08002
Tel: 93 318 62 00
Fax: 93 301 77 76
An old building that has been brought up-to-date with modern facilities including personal computers.

Allegro★★★
Avinguda Portal de l'Angel 17, 08002
Tel: 93 318 41 41
Fax: 93 301 26 31
A newcomer in the Old Town. This 19th-century palace has been well renovated to become an attractive modern hotel while retaining many original decorative features. There are peaceful rooms at the back with small terraces.

Colon★★★★
Avinguda de Catedral 7, 08002
Tel: 93 301 14 04
Fax: 93 317 29 15
The Colón is one of the city's best-known hotels. Facing the cathedral, it is an extremely comfortable place with a relaxed, old-world feel.

Continental★★★
La Rambla 138, 08002
Tel: 93 301 25 70
Fax: 93 302 73 60
Featured in Orwell's *Homage to Catalonia* – which is enough to attract many people – this is an eccentric hotel fully carpeted and wallpapered, but its individuality has charm and the rooms on La Rambla are in a prime position. All round good value.

Oriente★★★
Rambla 45–47, 08002
Tel: 93 302 25 58
Fax: 93 412 38 19
Built around a 17th-century monastic college, the Oriente has been a hotel for over a century. Good-sized rooms.

San Agustí★★★
Plaça de Sant Agustí 3, 08001
Tel: 93 318 16 58
Fax: 93 317 29 28
Attractive hotel in a pretty square off La Rambla. The best rooms are under the beams on the fourth floor and are well worth the extra cost.

España★★
Carrer de Sant Pau 9–11, 08001
Tel: 93 318 17 58
Fax: 93 317 11 34
This hotel has a beautiful Domènech i Montaner dining room, but unfortunately this is not matched by the bedrooms. The set menu lunch, amid the Modernist decor, is very good value.

Above: the state-of-the-art Arts Hotel

Hosteria Grau★★
Ramelleres, 27, 08001
Tel: 93 301 81 35
Fax: 93 317 68 25
On the basic side, but simple, clean and very reasonable. Only 5 minutes from airport bus terminal in Plaça de Catalunya and convenient for all parts of town.

Jardi★★
Sant Josep Oriol 1, 08002
Tel: 93 301 59 00
Fax: 93 318 36 64
One of the best-situated of the small hotels, the Jardí is also relatively inexpensive. Word has got around, so book early; ask for a room with a balcony.

Nouvel★★
Santa Ana 18–20, 08002
Tel: 93 301 82 74
Fax: 93 301 83 70
The Nouvel offers pleasant art nouveau surroundings, especially the dining room. Conveniently situated just off the Rambla.

Rialto★★
Carrer Ferrán 42
Tel: 93 318 52 12
Fax: 93 38 53 12
No frills but comfortable and clean in a pleasant street near Plaça Sant Jaume.

Peninsular★
Carrer de Sant Pau 34, 08001
Tel: 302 31 38
Fax: 412 36 99
Set in a former Augustinian monastery, with an attractive internal courtyard. Good value with lots of character and obliging staff.

Self Catering
There are a number of moderately priced self-catering establishments, including:
Access
Gran Via de les Corts Catalans
Tel: 93 425 51 61
Bertrán
Carrer Bertrán 150
Tel: 93 212 75 50
Senator
Via Augusta 167
Tel: 93 201 14 05

Central Booking
If you have trouble finding a hotel – and rooms do get booked well in advance – you could try contacting the central booking offices of some of the large hotel chains to see what accommodation is available:
Derby Hotels
Tel: 93 414 29 70
Guitart Hotels
Tel: 972 34 70 00
Hoteles Catalonia
Tel: 93 418 48 18
NH Hotels
Tel: 93 412 23 23

FURTHER READING

Catalan Cuisine, Colman Andrews. Headline. A lively and intelligent account of the region's food.
Barcelona Design Guide. Editorial Gustavo Gili SA. A handy pocket book giving the low-down on the city's centre for good design and the more stylish nightclubs, interiors, and shopping in general.
Barcelona: a Thousand Years of the City's Past, Felipe Fernandez-Armesto. Oxford University Press. A detailed and provocative view of the city by a non-Catalan.
Forbidden Territory, Juan Goytisolo. Quartet Books. An autobiography that gives great insight into the city during the years of Franco's dictatorship.
Barcelona, Robert Hughes. HarperCollins. An appraisal of the city and its culture by *Time* magazine's art critic.
Insight Compact Guide Barcelona, Jürgen Reiter. Apa Publications. Useful quick reference guide to the city's sights. Illustrated with colour photography and maps.
Insight Guide: Barcelona, Pam Barrett (ed). Apa Publications. A complete guide to the city, by local writers and journalists. Illustrated with Insight Guides' usual high quality photographs.
Insight Guide: Catalonia. Roger Williams (ed). Apa Publications. Incisive background features as well as a full run-down of sights and a detailed travel tips section.
Homage to Barcelona, Colm Tóibín. Simon & Schuster. An excellent award-winning account by this gifted Irish writer.

Right: a leisurely way to view the city's sights

ACKNOWLEDGEMENTS

Photography	**Annabel Elston** *and*
13	**AKG**
2/3	**J. D. Dallet**
7B, 27	**Jerry Dennis**
72	**Tor Eigland**
78	**Wolfgang Fritz**
45	**Andrew Holt**
61, 72	**Tor Eigeland**
10	**Jose Martin**
42, 67	**Mike Merchant**
29T	**Ingrid Morato**
5, 14, 32, 36, 39, 47, 50, 56, 61, 62, 66, 73, 74, 75, 77, 87	**Prisma Archivo Fotografico**
11	**Jan Read**
16	**Topham Picturepoint**
22T, 25B, 26T/B, 30T, 34B, 35, 43, 52, 58, 59, 63, 64T, 68, 76, 85, 90	**Bill Wassman**
1, 8/9, 15, 38, 48, 53, 60, 69	**Roger Williams**
82	**George Wright**
Cover	**Greg Balfour Evans**
Back Cover	**Annabel Elston**
Cartography	**Berndtson & Berndtson**

Left: the Magic Fountain casts its spell in front of the Palau Nacional

The travel guides that replace a tour guide – now better than ever with more listings and a fresh new design

INSIGHT
Pocket Guides

Insight Pocket Guides pioneered a new approach to guidebooks, introducing the concept of the authors as "local hosts" who would provide readers with personal recommendations, just as they would give honest advice to a friend who came to stay. They also included a full-size pull-out map.

Now, to cope with the needs of the 21st century, new editions in this growing series are being given a new look to make them more practical to use, and restaurant and hotel listings have been greatly expanded.

INSIGHT GUIDES

The world's largest collection of visual travel guides

Now in association with

Also from Insight Guides...

Insight Guides is the classic series, providing the complete picture with expert and informative text and stunning photography. Each book is an ideal travel planner, a reliable on-the-spot companion – and a superb visual souvenir of a trip. 193 titles.

Insight Maps are designed to complement the guidebooks. They provide full mapping of major destinations, and their laminated finish gives them ease of use and durability. 85 titles.

Insight Compact Guides are handy reference books, modestly priced yet comprehensive. The text, pictures and maps are all cross-referenced, making them ideal books to consult while seeing the sights. 119 titles.

Aegean Islands
Algarve
Alsace
Amsterdam
Athens
Atlanta
Bahamas
Baja Peninsula
Bali
Bali Bird Walks
Bangkok
Barbados
Barcelona
Bavaria
Beijing
Berlin
Bermuda
Bhutan
Boston
Brisbane & the
  Gold Coast
British Columbia
Brittany
Brussels

Budapest
California,
  Northern
Canton
Chiang Mai
Chicago
Corsica
Costa Blanca
Costa Brava
Costa Rica
Crete
Denmark
Fiji Islands
Florence
Florida
Florida Keys
French Riviera
  (Côte d'Azur)
Gran Canaria
Hawaii
Hong Kong
Hungary
Ibiza
Ireland
Ireland's

Southwest
Israel
Istanbul
Jakarta
Jamaica
Kathmandu Bikes
  & Hikes
Kenya
Kuala Lumpur
Lisbon
Loire Valley
London
Los Angeles
Macau
Madrid
Malacca
Maldives
Mallorca
Malta
Manila
Marbella
Melbourne
Mexico City
Miami
Montreal

Morocco
Moscow
Munich
Nepal
New Delhi
New Orleans
New York City
New Zealand
Oslo and
  Bergen
Paris
Penang
Perth
Phuket
Prague
Provence
Puerto Rico
Quebec
Rhodes
Rome
Sabah
St. Petersburg
San Francisco
Sarawak
Sardinia

Scotland
Seville, Cordoba &
  Granada
Seychelles
Sicily
Sikkim
Singapore
Southeast England
Southern Spain
Sri Lanka
Sydney
Tenerife
Thailand
Tibet
Toronto
Tunisia
Turkish Coast
Tuscany
Venice
Vienna
Vietnam
Yogjakarta
Yucatán Peninsula

INDEX